COLLECTING THE 20TH CENTURY

COLLECTING
THE 20TH CENTURY

EDITED BY FRANCES CAREY

Published for the Trustees of the British Museum by

BRITISH MUSEUM PRESS

© 1991 The Trustees of the British Museum

Published by British Museum Press
A division of British Museum
Publications Ltd
46 Bloomsbury Street
London WC1B 3QQ

British Library Cataloguing in
Publication Data
Collecting the 20th Century
  I. Carey, Frances
  709.41074

    ISBN 0 7141 1650 5

Designed by Roger Davies
Typeset and printed by BAS Printers
Limited, Over Wallop

The editor would like to thank the
authors of the individual chapters
and also the following curators for
their contributions:
(C&M) Philip Attwood, Virginia
Hewitt
(Ethno) John Mack, Brian Durrans,
Dorota Starzecka, Michael O'Hanlon,
Elizabeth Carmichael, Shelagh Weir,
Nigel Barley
(OA) Venetia Porter, Ann Farrer,
Richard Blurton, Jane Portal,
Shelagh Vainker
(MLA) David Thompson, John
Leopold.

The publishers would like to thank
the following photographers for their
contributions to this book: Paul
Gardner, David Gowers, Christi
Graham, Charles Howson, Dudley
Hubbard, Graham Javes, Ivor
Kerslake, Kevin Lovelock, James
Rossiter, John Williams.

Front cover: **Effigies of paper**,
representing a man and various
consumer durables, created by Koh
Ah Bah, and other Chinese, for use
in the *Kong Teik* funerary ceremony,
Penang, Malaysia, 1980s. Length of
bike: 1.75 m.

Replicas of motor bikes, telephones,
money, and other symbols of wordly
success are burnt by Chinese in
offering to recently deceased
relatives. When propitiated in this
way, with appropriate ritual
conducted by specialist priests, the
souls of the dead are believed to be
pacified during their passage
through limbo and purgatory. While
the artefacts represented are clearly
twentieth century in origin, the
elaborate ceremonies and attendant
beliefs link to older traditions
sustained up to the present day.

Ethno 1989 As 4

Back cover: **Porcelain plate**, painted
at the State Porcelain Factory,
Petrograd, Russia in 1920 after a
design created in 1919 by the artist
V P Belkin to commemorate the
second anniversary of the October
Revolution. Diameter 235 mm.

After the Russian revolution of
1917, the former Imperial Porcelain
Factory recruited many outstanding
artists to make new designs for
porcelain, to be used as a
propaganda tool. This plate, painted
with the dynamism of the Futurist
style, depicts factory buildings
billowing with smoke and framed
with red bands. The slogan reads
'The victory of the workers', while
the classical temple and the red star
symbolise the old order giving way
to the new Soviet State.

MLA 1981, 12–8, 2

Half title page: RONALD SEARLE
(b. 1920), **Study for reverse of medal**,
1973. Pen and black ink, 230 mm.
Presented by the artist.

The design shows 'La Gloire'
kneeling on the flat ground of
Cambridgeshire, Searle's native
landscape, ready to crown the artist
whose self-portrait appeared on the
front of the medal struck in bronze in
1975. It was the first of a series
commissioned by the French Mint on
the history of caricature. The British
Museum owns a complete set of the
medals and thirty-six of the
preparatory drawings.

PD 1983-6-25-55

Frontispiece: DAVID SMITH (1906–
1965). **Untitled**, 1951. Oil and
gouache, 665 × 504 mm.

The American artist, David Smith, is
known as one of the foremost
abstract sculptors of the twentieth
century. Painting and drawing also
played a major role throughout his
career as parallel means of exploring
certain ideas, rather than as direct
preparatory studies for sculpture.

PD 1988-10-1-44

Contents page: **Lime spatula**,
Trobriand Islands, Milne Bay
Province, Papua New Guinea. Early
twentieth century. L: 250 mm.
Donated by Mrs H G Beasley.

Lime spatulae are part of the
equipment for chewing 'betel nut'
(actually the nut of the areca palm)
in this area. Their handles constitute
a miniature Milne Bay art form, and
are carved with representations of
birds, animals and canoes in
addition to the human figures.

Ethno. 1944 Oc.2.1901

NORMAN BEL GEDDES (1898–1958),
**25th Anniversary of General
Motors**, American medal, 1933.
Struck silver, 76 mm.
Presented by General Motors
Corporation.

In this medal, the industrial designer
Bel Geddes has dispensed with
traditional symbols of speed,
choosing instead to express the past
and future of the car in a modernist
idiom. The future is represented by
the generalised streamlined form
symbolising 'ultimate efficiency in
speed'; on the back of the medal (not
shown) the past is evoked by the
combustion chamber (described by
the artist as 'the heart of the car').

CM 1934-6-2-2

Contents

Preface

This publication brings together for the first time the many different results of the British Museum's active pursuit of twentieth-century material, which ranges from ethnographic field-work, exchanges with institutions abroad and close collaboration with private donors and artists, to purchase on the open market across the world. The expertise and enthusiasm of six curatorial departments have combined to provide a substantial basis for the collections of the next century. The Trustees, the British Museum Society, the Contemporary Art Society, the National Art Collections Fund and private individuals have contributed the wherewithal for the acquisitions while the Patrons of the museum have generously paid for this publication. The greatest debt of all, however, is owed to the Director, Sir David Wilson, who, from the very beginning of his tenure in 1977 appreciated the importance of carrying the collections forward so that the vitality and relevance of the British Museum should be sustained for the future. It is to him, therefore, that *Collecting the 20th Century*, the book and the exhibition (October 3, 1991–February 16, 1992) are dedicated on his retirement at the end of 1991.

Frances Carey

Introduction

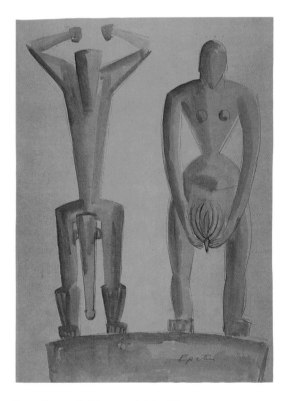

JACOB EPSTEIN (1880–1959), **Man Woman**, c. 1913.
Pencil and red wash, 567 × 413 mm.

Epstein formed an outstanding collection of sculpture,
embracing Ancient Egyptian, Cycladic, African, Oceanic,
Pre-Columbian and North American Indian material.
Man Woman is related to the figures on the top of a
mortuary post from Madagascar which he subsequently
acquired.

PD 1980–11–8–4

'The present is burthened too much with the past.
We have not time . . . to appreciate what is warm
with life, and immediately around us; yet we
heap up all these old shells, out of which human
life has long emerged, casting them off forever.
I do not see how future ages are to stagger under
all this dead weight, with the additions that will
continually be made to it.'[1] This sense of
intimidation before the sheer volume of antiquity
housed within the British Museum which the
American writer, Nathaniel Hawthorne, expressed in 1856, has doubtless been shared by many
for whom the institution is entirely associated
with a remote past, from its Greek Revival building to the very names of its departmental collections, all but three of which are still designated
as 'antiquities'. The purpose of this publication,
however, is to demonstrate the strength of the
museum's commitment to the modern as well as
to the ancient world, within the context of
representing as comprehensive a history as possible of the development of all cultures. The
extent to which this universality has been
observed over nearly 250 years has been affected
by many factors: the accidents of gift and bequest,
the changing assumptions of contemporary collecting, the rise of other public collections, the
interests of successive members of staff and, not
least of all, the financial constraints under which
the museum has laboured.

From its foundation in 1753 as the first
national museum in the world to be both public
and secular, the British Museum has always
included contemporary artefacts. This was at the
outset a consequence of the eclecticism of Sir
Hans Sloane's 'cabinet of curiosities' from which
the museum began, and of its unique position as
a national collection, attracting a very hetero-
geneous assortment of gifts. As Horace Walpole,
one of the museum's first Trustees, wrote in
1757: 'Who that should destine his collection to
the British museum, would not purchase curiosities with redoubled spirit and pleasure, whenever
he reflected, that he was collecting for his
country, and would have his name recorded as
a benefactor to its arts and improvements?'[2] For
an enterprising manufacturer in the late
eighteenth century with an eye to posterity, like
Josiah Wedgwood, the British Museum proved an

HENRI GAUDIER-BRZESKA (1891–1915), **Head of a Japanese Girl**, 1912–13. Coloured chalks, 310 × 375 mm.

One of a group of vividly coloured pastel portraits executed at this time, which reflects Gaudier-Brzeska's interest in different physiognomic types as well as Japanese prints. It was originally owned by the theatrical designer, Claud Lovat Fraser (1890–1921), one of Gaudier's first patrons in London.

PD 1971–2–27–1

invaluable quarry for designs after its acquisition of Sir William Hamilton's collection of Greek vases in 1772. As a result, Wedgwood claimed that within two years he had been able to bring into the country about three times the sum expended on the purchase of the collection and in 1786 he presented to the British Museum the Pegasus Vase, designed by John Flaxman, as 'the finest and most perfect I have ever made.'[3] Of great consequence for the future development of the collections was the ethnographic material gathered from Captain Cook's three voyages to the Pacific 1767–1779, the first selection of which was presented by the Admiralty in 1775 to be displayed 'as a monument of these national exertions of British munificence and industry'.[4] The objects were exhibited in Montagu House in what became known as the 'Otaheiti or South Sea Room', where after 1808 the display was broadened 'to illustrate particular Customs of different Nations; their Religion, their Government, their Commerce, Manufactures or Trades.'[5]

In the course of the nineteenth century the collections were organised on a more systematic basis and parliamentary attention was turned to the proper objectives of the British Museum.

Coins, medals and prints were collected without chronological delimitation on typological and iconographical grounds as well as in relation to the development of their respective techniques. The Keeper of Prints and Drawings from 1845–1866, W H Carpenter, was aware of the importance of bringing the collection up to date; in his evidence of 1848 to the Royal Commission on the British Museum, he expressed his desire to set aside £200 out of his annual grant of £1200 for the purchase of modern prints, subsequently using it to good effect, for example, in the acquisition of prints after J M W Turner and the early etchings of Manet. The antiquities collections beyond the classical period lacked such a readily definable sense of purpose but in 1860 a distinction was articulated between the archaeological scope of the British Museum (where the material was perceived as being selected 'on the principle of illustrating the history of a period, and of a country, and of the men producing the object'[6] and the more purely aesthetic criteria used in the formation of the collection of decorative art at the newly-founded South Kensington Museum.

The existence of the latter institution, which was renamed the Victoria and Albert Museum

HENRY MOORE (1898–1986), **Crowd Looking at a Tied-up Object,** 1942. Watercolour over coloured chalks, 400 × 550 mm.

The main source for Moore's most famous pictorial composition was probably an illustration in Leo Frobenius' influential book of 1933, *Kulturgeschichte Africas*. The reproduction shows Nupe tribesmen from Northern Nigeria standing around two veiled Dako cult dance costumes. *Crowd Looking at a Tied-up Object* was one of nine drawings from the estate of Lord Clark allocated to the British Museum in lieu of Capital Transfer Tax.

PD 1988-3-5-7

in 1899, had a considerable influence on the direction taken by the British Museum in its acquisitions policy. Augustus Wollaston Franks, Keeper of the Department of British and Medieval Antiquities and Ethnography from 1866–96, who did so much to expand the collections in the post-classical European, Islamic and Far Eastern fields, seems nevertheless to have regarded objects of contemporary manufacture as being largely the province of the V&A.[7] This attitude persisted until well into the twentieth century,

when it was reinforced by an inherent conservatism which came to equate modernism with the ephemeral fashions of a dubious avant-garde in Europe and the adulteration and decline of indigenous cultures the world over. The painter and designer, Paul Nash, touched upon these issues when he wrote in 1933: 'Whether it is possible to "go modern" and still "be British" is a question vexing quite a few people today ... The battle lines have been drawn up: internationalism versus an indigenous culture; renovation versus conservatism; the industrial versus the pastoral; the functional versus the futile.'[8]

No collecting policy, however, should be immutable nor should missed opportunities in the past be advanced as a reason for inactivity in the present. The final quarter of the twentieth century has witnessed a reassessment of the British Museum's responsibility towards the history of mankind as a whole. In the light of this re-evaluation a variety of new initiatives have been taken which are described here under the different departmental headings of Coins and Medals, Ethnography, Oriental Antiquities, Japanese Antiquities, Medieval and Later Antiquities and Prints and Drawings. These divisions are the result of frequent shifts in alignment since the museum's foundation which have influenced the shape of the different collections. Until 1933, for example, Chinese and Japanese paintings and prints formed part of the Prints and Drawings Department, which in turn was affected by the close proximity of the library collections until their administrative separation from the British Museum in 1973; Medieval and Later Antiquities emerged from the *omnium gatherum* Department of Antiquities in the nineteenth century and now encompasses all artefacts of the Christian world from Byzantium to the latter half of the twentieth century. The diversity of the British Museum's range of endeavour precludes the development of a unitary policy of acquisition applicable to every field, each of which has thus its own history and momentum and stands in varying relationships to collections elsewhere. Ethnography and Coins and Medals pursue a more comprehensively documentary approach than their colleagues because of the dearth of equivalent collections in these areas, whereas the Oriental departments, Medieval and Later Antiquities and Prints and Drawings must partly address themselves to complementing the holdings of the V&A, the British Library, the National Portrait Gallery and the Tate Gallery, with reference also to the Imperial War Museum and the Museum of London among others. The resultant situation among the national museums is not one with rigid lines of demarcation or needless duplication but a more fluid set of relationships, betokening a plurality of approach and contextualization which can be

as beneficial to the collection of twentieth-century material as it is for earlier periods.

The broad spectrum embraced by the British Museum means that twentieth-century material is seen as part of an historical continuum in relation to the different cultures from which it has emerged. This deference to individual integrities does not, however, ignore the realities of the contemporary situation when 'identities no longer presuppose continuous cultures or traditions. Everywhere individuals and groups improvise local performances from (re)collected pasts, drawing on foreign media, symbols and languages.'[9] Notions of modernity vary enormously among the different cultures represented in the museum. In European eyes, artistic modernism tends to be seen as synonymous with an anti-traditionalist, progressive avant-garde; when traditional forms and techniques are perpetuated, such repetition is frequently derided as mere 'pastiche' or 'imitation'. These assumptions are not common to non-European cultures, which in some cases explicitly revere the imitation of past styles and in others make little distinction between the old and the new. Modernity, moreover, is something Europeans are prone to distrust in other societies, seeking to impose an artificial standard of 'authenticity' on their material culture which denies them the right of change and assimilation. Europeans, on the other hand, have themselves been especially quick in the present century to appropriate the outward forms of alien cultures for their own artistic purposes. The French sculptor, Henri Gaudier-Brzeska, who settled in London at the beginning of 1911, was one of many to be moved by the emotional force of 'pagan' art (whether Classical, Oriental or 'tribal') to declare in 1910 that he was 'finished with Ruskin and the English . . . and Christian philosophy',[10] subsequently turning to Hindu, African and Polynesian sculpture, Japanese prints and sword hilts for inspiration. Museum collections were of crucial importance to this expanding frame of reference among the artistic communities of Paris, Dresden, Berlin, New York and London, where the British Museum played a significant part in the development of sculptors like Gaudier-Brzeska, Jacob Epstein, Leon Underwood, Henry

EDUARDO PAOLOZZI (b. 1924),
British Museum Tapis, 1950.
Brush and black ink,
358 × 479 mm.

The subject was inspired by either
the embroidered design on a type of
warp-ikat tapis cloth from
Southern Sumatra or a painted
bark cloth from the Northern
Philippines which Paolozzi would
have seen among the ethnographic
displays at the British Museum.
The exhibition, *Lost Magic
Kingdoms*, held at the Museum of
Mankind in 1985, was selected by
Paolozzi to illuminate the whole
process by which the forms and
ideas he has borrowed from other
cultures are re-invented within his
own artistic framework.
PD 1990-5-19-10

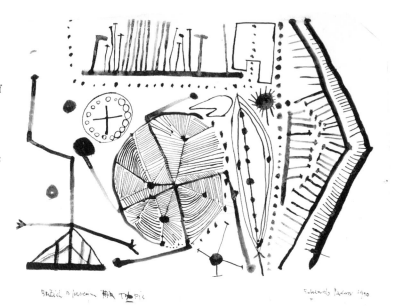

Moore and Eduardo Paolozzi as well as countless others who were only occasional visitors to London. The American sculptor, David Smith, came to the British Museum at the end of his first visit to Europe in May 1936, where he was moved by the mordancy of the German World War I medals on display to execute his own series of 'Medals for Dishonor' 1937–40, after his return to the United States.

The impact of the British Museum's collections on successive generations of writers, artists and designers is part of the dynamic of its relationship with the present, a dynamic which is sustained by its involvement with twentieth-century acquisitions. The accumulation of material thus continues unabated, since the museum is defined by its role as a reference and lending collection of infinite resource as well as by its public display galleries. The present is, no doubt, destined to be forever 'burthened too much with the past' in the British Museum but henceforth that past will at least stand in greater adjacency to the present.

Frances Carey

References

1 Nathaniel Hawthorne, *The English Notebooks*, ed Randall Stewart, OUP, London 1941, p 294, entry for March 27th, 1856.

2 'Advertisement to a Catalogue and Description of King Charles the First's Collections' quoted by Mrs K A Esdaile in *The Life and Works of Louis François Roubiliac*, OUP, London 1928, p 103

3 Letter to Sir William Hamilton 27 June 1786, quoted by Aileen Dawson in *Masterpieces of Wedgwood in the British Museum* BMP, London 1984, p 106.

4 Edward Miller, *That Noble Cabinet*, André Deutsch, London 1973, p 75.

5 Miller, *op cit*, p 221.

6 *Report from the Select Committee on the British Museum* 1860, p 182.

7 For an account of Franks as a collector see Sir David Wilson, *The Forgotten Collector*, sixteenth Walter Neurath Memorial Lecture, Thames and Hudson, London 1984.

8 'Going Modern and Being British', *The Weekend Review*, 12 March 1933, pp 322–3. I am indebted to Andrew Stephenson of University College, London, for drawing my attention to this article.

9 James Clifford, *The Predicament of Culture*, Harvard University Press, Cambridge, Mass, 1988, p 14.

10 H S Ede, *Savage Messiah*, William Heinemann, London, 1931, p 19.

Coins and Medals

In May 1695 Ralph Thoresby noted that the naturalist William Courten possessed 'the most noble collection of natural and artificial curiosities, of ancient and modern coins and medals that any private person in the world enjoys'.

It was this collection, bequeathed by Courten to Sir Hans Sloane in 1702, which, with Sloane's subsequent additions and the smaller collections from the Harley and Cotton libraries, came into the charge of Andrew Gifford, the British Museum's first numismatist, in 1757.

Ancient coins (or medals as they were generally called) were highly prized by antiquarians of the period as the most reliable source of historical evidence about the distant past and as an unrivalled source for the likenesses of famous individuals. The creators and collectors of modern medals, and coins, regarded them in the same light, as the surest way of documenting and immortalising the features of individuals and the important events with which they were connected.

E Powlett's 1761 guidebook to the British Museum describes displays of English, French and Italian medals, which recorded Popes and monarchs from the Middle Ages to the present day. It was a feature of each of these exhibits that they ended with the present ruler, displaying a desire to document the present as well as the past which was also evident in each of the three major collections, of C M Cracherode, Miss S S Banks and George III, which came to the museum in the late eighteenth and early nineteenth century.

Sarah Sophia, sister of Sir Joseph Banks, was a particularly enthusiastic collector of coins, tokens and medals which related to contemporary events. Political medals and tokens of the period were made in large numbers, provided instant comment on the affairs of the moment and were frequently worn as a sign of loyalty to one cause or another. Twentieth-century political badges, several thousand of which have been acquired by the British Museum over the last decade, are, in function at least, the contemporary equivalent of the pieces that Miss Banks acquired, hot from the press, two hundred years ago. Like them they will provide future generations with a concise, yet highly evocative summary of changing political and social attitudes.

PIOTR GAWRON (b. 1943), **Collector**, Polish medal, 1985. Cast bronze, partly enamelled, 132 × 105 mm.

Since the Second World War medallic art has been particularly strong in Eastern Europe, with Hungary, Czechoslovakia and Poland making significant contributions. Here, Warsaw sculptor Piotr Gawron provides an unsettling image of the collector, his collection of female portraits strung around his neck on leather thongs.

CM 1985-12-35-1

Joseph Gangl, **1914**, German medal, 1914.
Cast iron, partly gilt, 100 mm. Presented by Mr M
Frankenhuis.

The First World War witnessed a remarkable increase in
medallic activity in Germany. Gangl's medals carry
propaganda messages, but also point to the horror of
war. The bloody sword on this sombre reverse presages
the impending slaughter, while the German eagle
attached to the blade proclaims the expected German
victory.

CM 1919–6–10–42

Andrew Gifford's successors, most notably
Edward Hawkins (Keeper of Antiquities 1826–
60), were keen collectors of medals illustrating
British history. The acquisition of Hawkins' own
collection, in 1860, and the subsequent efforts
of A W Franks (who found time to work on
British medals even though he was Keeper of
another department) and H A Grueber (appointed 1866, retired 1912) ensured that the British
Museum's collection remained up-to-date. Both
retained a belief in the documentary importance
of coins and medals and were therefore concerned to acquire any object, however unattrac-
tive or commonplace, which might have some
historical significance.

This approach was, however, going out of
fashion. Students of Greek coins had begun to
place increasing emphasis on their value as

The Sinking of the Lusitania
Top German medal by Karl Goetz (1875–1950), 1915.
Cast iron, 55 mm. Presented by Mr H van den Bergh.
Bottom British medal, 1915. Cast iron, 55 mm.
Presented by Sir G F Hill.

Goetz was one of the most prolific artists to contribute to
the remarkable flowering of medallic activity in Germany
in the years around the First World War.

The sinking of the transatlantic liner off the south west
coast of Ireland in May 1915 was the catalyst for
America's entry into the war. This Goetz medal criticises
the 'Business above all' attitude of Cunard; a skeleton
continues to sell tickets, undeterred by the newspaper
headline warning of 'U-Boat danger'. The German claim
that the *Lusitania* was engaged in war work is underlined
by the presence of artillery, and even an aircraft, on
board the sinking ship. Copies of Goetz's medal were
produced in England in large numbers, and distributed
to show that 'such crimes . . . are given every
encouragement in the land of Kultur'. The counter-
propaganda was so effective that in 1917 manufacture
of the original medal was forbidden in Germany.

CM 1916–7–7–9

CM 1917–5–3–1

KARL GOETZ (1875–1950), **Hoarders,** German medal, 1916. Cast bronze, 58 mm. Presented by Mr M Frankenhuis.

The medal criticises the system whereby big racketeers might move trainloads of goods freely whereas small-time hoarders ran the risk of being searched and losing everything. While many of Goetz's wartime medals are propaganda pieces, others such as this highlight social iniquities and display a genuine concern for the individual.

CM 1920–2–33–21

SIDNEY CARLINE (1888–1929), **Battle of Jutland**, British medal, 1916. Cast bronze, 84 mm.

The lacklustre response of British medallists to the First World War was in direct contrast to the vitality of German medallic art. A competition for a medal to commemorate the Battle of Jutland was intended to rectify this. Carline's medal, although unplaced in the competition, is undoubtedly the most original British contribution of the time in this medium.

CM 1979–12–27–2

KARL GOETZ (1875–1950), **The Border itself turns against Poland**, German medal, 1921. Cast bronze, 59 mm.

This medal protests against the transferral of Upper Silesia to Poland in accordance with the Treaty of Versailles, despite a 1921 plebiscite in which the majority of the population voted in favour of remaining within Germany. The outline of the province is transformed into an angry human profile confronting Poland.

CM 1990–11–6–5

works of art. The *Catalogue of Greek coins: Sicily*, for example, published in 1874, used such terms as 'period of finest art' and 'period of decline', as the basic structure for classification of the material in question, and it was the artistic quality of contemporary coins and medals that came increasingly to interest its authors R S Poole (appointed 1852, retired 1893) and B V Head (appointed 1864, retired 1906). In collaboration with Charles Fremantle, the Deputy Master of the Royal Mint, Sidney Colvin, Keeper of Prints and Drawings at the British Museum and artists like Sir Frederick Leighton and Edward Poynter, Poole even founded a 'Society of Medallists' devoted to 'the encouragement and cultivation of the art of making medals'. Poole, Head, and above all Sir George Hill (appointed 1893, retired 1936) were all actively concerned to raise the standard of contemporary medallic art and coin design and acquired, often by gift

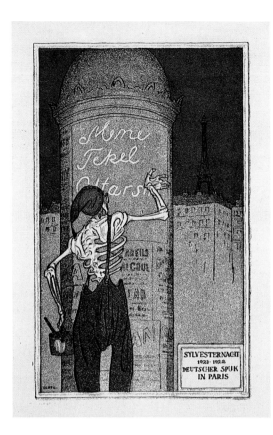

75 Pfennig note, Kahla, Germany, 1921.
127 × 86 mm. Presented by Mrs Furryan-Fisher.

Small-denomination notes issued in German towns
during and immediately after World War I often carried
stark wartime propaganda. In this grisly example, the
skeletal spectre of Germany stalks the streets of Paris,
inscribing a pillar with the Biblical warning from
Belshazzar's feast: 'Mene, Tekel, Upharsin', ie 'thy days
are numbered . . .'.
CM 1961–6–9–633

from the artist, numerous medals created as
works of art. Hill, famous for his work on medals
of the Italian renaissance, had a lively interest in
contemporary work. Despite his professed loath-
ing of all things German he acquired an
extremely fine collection of World War I German
medals over the years 1915–20 and it was his
exhibition of these medals, mounted in the
1920s, which inspired the sculptor David Smith's
'Medals for Dishonor' in the late 1930s.

Hill, however, abandoned systematic acquisition of cheap, popular medals and his immediate
successors did not share his interest in medallic
art. It was not until the late 1960s that another
Greek numismatist, G K Jenkins, began once
again to acquire medals as contemporary art. In
the last 15 years, under Sir David Wilson, the
museum has begun systematically to fill the late
nineteenth and twentieth-century gaps in the
documentary collections of coins and medals and
to build a representative collection of contemporary medallic art.

Some of the best examples come, not from the
guardians of the great tradition, like Italy and
France, but from Eastern Europe and in particular Poland, Hungary, Czechoslovakia and East
Germany. In these countries the political and
economic problems of working on a large scale
have led hundreds of sculptors to use medal-
making as a primary vehicle for the expression
of their artistic and political concerns. The fall of
the Berlin Wall in November 1989 evoked an
immediate response from artists in both East and
West Germany, whose work in this context has
already been acquired by the British Museum.

In Britain, by contrast, medals had, in the post-
war period, come to be seen as a marginal form
of artistic activity. Over the past decade, however,
this has begun to change, partly as a result of the
efforts of the British Art Medal Society, a
modern equivalent of the Society of Medallists,
which has had some success in reviving interest
in medal-making among contemporary artists.

It is also due to Sir David Wilson that, in a
single decade, the British Museum's collection of
paper money has grown from a modest and
randomly acquired assortment to a position of
international eminence. Bank-notes, like coins,
are essential to any understanding of the history
of money. Like medals they can, as German Notgeld demonstrate, be visually exciting and, as the
most official of images, they provide a carefully
conceived self-portrait of the societies that produce them.

Underlying these new departures in collecting
policy is a renewed respect for the documentary
value of objects and a return to the open-minded
and universalist attitudes that marked the first
century of the British Museum's existence. It is

German Notgeld
Top left **100 Pfennig**, Gustrow, 1922.
104 × 69 mm. Presented by Mr H Pirie-Gordon.
Top right **50 Pfennig**, Hameln, 1922. 96 × 64 mm.
Bottom **75 Pfennig**, Erfurt, 1921. 94 × 72 mm;
both presented by Mrs Furryan-Fisher.

These brightly-coloured notes for low sums were first
issued to provide small change during the war. However,
they soon became collectors' items and were often
produced in series with local themes. The example from
Hameln illustrates the legend of the Pied Piper.

CM 1957–7–1–68

CM 1961–6–9–127

CM 1961–6–9–405

Note for 100 Griven, Ukraine, 1918. 175 × 115 mm.

East European notes from the early twentieth century are
often distinguished by romantic stylised designs with a
floral theme. In this striking example, figures
representing agriculture and labour stand by a garland
of fruits, grains and flowers, all the riches of the soil.
During the Russian Civil War both independent states,
like the Ukraine, and internal factions issued their own
notes.

CM 1984–6–5–1817

also a return to the long view which enabled late-
eighteenth-century collectors to amass contemporary material in the hope that it would be
of as much interest to subsequent generations as
the relics of ancient Rome and medieval Europe
were to them.

Mark Jones

IAN HAMILTON FINLAY (b. 1925), **Four British medals.**
Top **Emden**, 1976. Struck silver, 47 × 75 mm.
Left **Enterprise**, 1975. Struck copper, 38 mm.
Bottom **Thunderbolt**, 1975. Struck copper,
30 × 45 mm.
Right **Midway**, 1975. Struck copper, 38 mm.

From the 1970s military motifs have played an
important role in the art of the Scottish poet, sculptor and
gardener, Ian Hamilton Finlay. The *Emden* plaquette is a
homage to the solitary German light cruiser which did
much damage to Allied shipping at the beginning of the
First World War. The inscription, hingeing on the word
Kreuzer (cruiser), invites comparison with the virtuoso
soloist to whom Beethoven dedicated his celebrated
sonata.

The *Enterprise* medal shows the American aircraft
carrier as unifier of the elements. In his accompanying
text, Stephen Bann has written: 'Earth is the landing
ground offered by the carrier, air the element in which
its aircraft move, fire its dynamic and destructive
capacity and water the surrounding medium'.

Thunderbolt is an example of the subtle relationship
between image and inscription that has engaged
medallists since the Renaissance. On this 'heroic emblem'
the words are those of the ancient Greek philosopher
Heraclitus, with the tank as the modern equivalent of the
destructive power of the thunderbolt.

The complex *Midway* medal refers to the Battle of
Midway, fought by the American and Japanese fleets in
1942. Bursts of anti-aircraft fire evoke the dark wood of
the opening lines of the *Divine Comedy*. Dante's mid-life
becomes here the Midway, and a turning point of the war
– and indeed of modern warfare.

CM 1981–7–17–1
CM 1981–7–19–2
CM 1981–7–19–1
CM 1981–7–19–3

OTTO MACZEK, **Berlin Olympics, 1936**, German medal,
1936. Cast bronze, 70 mm.

Maczek is a little-known artist who produced a small
masterpiece in his medal commemorating the 1936
Berlin Olympics, which were most notably recorded in
Leni Riefenstahl's film *Olympische Spiele*. The row of
athletes, representing 'die Jugend der Welt' are portrayed
schematically, the parallel lines creating a dynamism
particularly appropriate to the event celebrated.

CM 1980–12–24–1

BERND GÖBEL (b. 1942), **For Felix**, German medal, 1987.
Cast bronze, 90 mm.

The medal is dedicated to the son of this East German
artist. A quotation from Heine on the other side refers to
the suffering of the present, but the imagery on the front,
a premonition of subsequent political events, offers hope
for the future in the form of a romantic landscape viewed
through a partially dismantled wall.

CM 1988–10–23–3

ROGER BEZOMBES (b. 1913), **Rouletabille**, French medal, 1970. Cast bronze with ball-bearings, 73 mm.

Bezombes was foremost amongst those artists who, in the 1960s, brought radically new ideas to medallic art. Arresting images result from his practice of incorporating natural or ready-made objects – shells, glass beads, or, as here, ball-bearings (*roulements à billes*) – into his designs.

CM 1977–8–14–6

DHRUVA MISTRY (b. 1957), **Maya medallion – the Dark One**, British medal, 1988. Cast bronze, 127 mm.

Mistry was born in India, and it was there that he first trained as a sculptor before making his home in Britain. In his sculptures, Indian themes fuse with European influences. In this, his only medal, the artist has interpreted *Maya* as 'illusion, dream or mirage . . . enchantment'.

CM 1989–3–5–1

Top JULES FEIFFER (b. 1929), **We are all prisoners of war**, American button badge, 1971. 44 mm.

This protest against the Vietnam War by the celebrated cartoonist stressed that all Americans were victims of the war. Simplicity and clarity, qualities to be found in the best political cartoons, are equally important in badge design, where the swift communication of a message is the aim.

CM 1986–4–17–1

Bottom JULES FEIFFER (b. 1929), **They lie**, American button badge, 1981. 53 mm.

The incorporation here of the image into the text is a fine example of Feiffer's economy of means. With two short words and a rough sketch of a cooling tower with radioactive clouds above, the artist conveys an immediately comprehensible attack on official obfuscation over nuclear power. This badge was produced by the Labor Committee for Safe Energy and Full Employment of Harrisburg, Pennsylvania two years after the near-meltdown of the reactor at Three Mile Island.

CM 1987–11–35–515

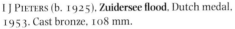

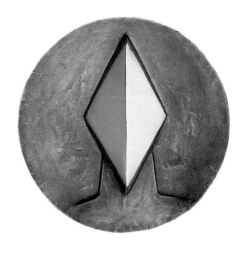

I J PIETERS (b. 1925), **Zuidersee flood**, Dutch medal, 1953. Cast bronze, 108 mm.

In Pieters' dramatic response to the floods of 1953, the waters engulf the house and in effect submerge the entire surface of the medal. The fragility of existence in the low-lying lands is vividly conveyed by the simplest of means. On the other side of the medal the dykes are being repaired.

CM 1985–8–3–9

LYNN CHADWICK (b. 1914), **Diamond**, British medal, 1984. Struck bronze, 75 mm.

This is the only medallic work by Chadwick. It relates closely to his large-scale sculptures, as, for example, the *Three Elektras* of 1969 and the pair of seated figures also entitled *Diamond* of 1984. The medal resulted from a commission from the British Art Medal Society.

CM 1984–12–2–1

Reserve Bank of Australia, 10 dollar note, 1988. 156 × 78 mm. Lent by the Reserve Bank of Australia.

Designs on contemporary notes often celebrate their country's history. This note, issued to commemorate the bicentennial of the first European settlers arriving in Australia, portrays an Aboriginal youth with elements of Aboriginal culture. For security, the note is printed on plastic, and includes a sophisticated hologram in the top right-hand corner.

CM 1988–8–27–1

Ethnography

Contemporary metal shield Wahgi people, Western Highlands Province, Papua New Guinea. H: 1.53 m. Purchased with the assistance of the B M Society.

The recent introduction of guns into local intergroup fighting has led some Wahgi men to replace wooden shields with metal ones made from car bodies. Decoration on contemporary shields is also innovatory, sometimes featuring the name of the shield-carrier – in this instance Kunump, whose reputed strength is recognized in the designations 'Superman' and 'Bulldozer'. At the same time, aspects of contemporary shield decoration, such as the border of red triangles, allude to traditional taboos on association with enemies.

This example was painted by Kaipel Ka ('KK'), a talented local signwriter whose novel designs appear on many Wahgi shields. He discreetly advertises his business at Talu near the base of the shield.

Ethno. 1990.Oc.9.18

The Department of Ethnography was created as a separate department within the British Museum in 1946, after 140 years of gradual development from the original Department of Antiquities. It is concerned with the peoples of Africa, the Americas, Asia, the Pacific and parts of Europe. While this includes complex kingdoms, as in Africa, and ancient empires, such as those of the Americas, the primary focus of attention in the twentieth century has been on small-scale societies, whether or not they have been influenced by major world religions or characterised by the use of written languages. Through its collections, the Department's specific interest is to document how objects are created and used, and to understand their importance and significance to those who produce them. Such objects can include both the extraordinary and the mundane, the beautiful and the banal.

The collections of the Department of Ethnography include approximately 300,000 artefacts, of which about half are the product of the present century. Notable field collections in the first half of the century were made in Central Africa and Belize, particularly at the behest of Captain T A Joyce, who was in charge of the Sub-Department of Ethnography 1933–38. However, the vast majority of early twentieth-century acquisitions derive from two sources: early anthropologists, colonial administrators and missionaries who worked in the field; and United Kingdom-based collectors such as Sir Henry Wellcome (1853–1936), the pharmaceutical manufacturer who came originally from Wisconsin.

The Department has a vital role to play in providing information on non-Western cultures to visitors and scholars. To this end, the collecting emphasis has often been less on individual objects than on groups of material which allow the display of a broad range of a society's cultural expressions. Thus, during the last fifteen years, the Department of Ethnography has acquired more than 25,000 artefacts in little more than 1,200 separate accessions. To give one instance, in a year such as 1985 two collections were acquired each week: one from the Americas, and a second from Asia, Africa or the Pacific. Stark figures give little idea of the aesthetic, technical and cultural variety of these collections – almost

Polychrome figure from Wosera Spirit House, East Sepik Province, Papua New Guinea. 1970s. H: 1.55 m.

Carved and painted figures are amongst the ritual furnishing of Wosera Spirit Houses, whose facades tower over local settlements. This figure represents a clan spirit or another being in Wosera cosmology.

Ethno. 1980.Oc.11.87

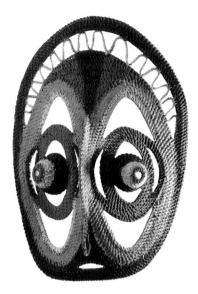

Basketry yam mask, Wosera people, East Sepik Province, Papua New Guinea. 1970s. H: 340 mm.

Male prestige in traditional Wosera society revolves around the competitive growing of long yams. Such yams, which are credited with certain human characteristics, are decorated with painted basketry masks, ceremonially displayed, and then presented by the grower to his exchange partner. Prestige accrues to the grower of the longest yams.

Ethno. 1980.Oc.11.209

all of which are of twentieth-century origin.

Much of this more recent collecting was carried out in the field, sometimes by museum staff working on general anthropological projects in collaboration with a wide variety of national governments and other institutions. The material collected includes great technical series – for instance, of textiles from Bolivia, Guatemala, Indonesia and areas of West Africa – or of artefact types such as boats. The latter include working examples of coracles from India, reed boats from Lake Titicaca in the Andes, kayaks from the Arctic, an outrigger canoe from Madagascar, and dug-out canoes from several countries. The field assemblages, such as those from the Sudan, Madagascar and Yemen, include a whole range of material culture representative of one people. This might cover the necessities of life of an African cattle herdsman or an Arabian farmer, ritual paraphernalia, or even on occasion airport art. Again, a series of accessions might represent a decade's fieldwork documenting social experience as expressed in the varieties of clothing and jewellery styles, tents and camel trappings from various Middle Eastern countries, or in the developing preferences in personal adornment and dress from the Highlands of Papua New Guinea. Particularly interesting are series of collections which continue to document the evolution of ceremony and of material forms for which the Department already possesses early (if not the earliest) collections formed after the first contact with Europeans. In Melanesia such series start in the nineteenth century with assemblages from explorers, and continue with the collections of early anthropologists such as A C Haddon, Bronislaw Malinowski, and during the 1930s Lord Moyne. In the 1960s and 1980s departmental staff continued this tradition. While an accession may contain thousands of artefacts, it may also consist of a single item: a complete wood house from Madagascar, or a needle case from the Copper Inuit. Similarly, collections may come from the urban artisans of Latin America or from people miscategorised in the past as marginal – the tropical forest dwellers, and the peoples from the world's ever-expanding arid regions in Africa, Asia and South America.

The importance of these acquisitions extends beyond the objects themselves. They come to the museum with documentation of their social context, ideally including photographic records. Such acquisitions have multiple purposes. Most significantly they document for future generations art and material culture (often of an ephemeral nature) in a world of accelerating change. Most people think of the cultures represented in the collection in terms of the absence of advanced technology. In fact, traditional practices draw on a continuing wealth of technological ingenuity. Limited resources and ecological constraints are often overcome by personal skills that would be regarded as exceptional in the West. Of

growing interest is the way in which much of what we might see as disposable is, elsewhere, recycled and reused.

With the decolonisation of much of Asia and Africa after 1945, it was assumed that economic progress would rapidly lead to the disappearance or assimilation of many small-scale societies. Therefore, it was felt that the Museum should acquire materials representing people whose art or material culture, ritual or political structures were on the point of irrevocable change. This attitude altered with the realisation that

VICTOR JUPURRULA ROSS, **Bush Potato Dreaming**, c. 1987. Yuendemu, Northern Territory, Australia. Acrylic paint on canvas, 1.59 × 1.60 m.

Over the last two decades, Aboriginal artists from central Australia have reproduced ancestrally important Dreamtime designs for sale on canvas. The first canvases from Yuendemu were sold to buy Toyota vehicles which enabled the painters to visit their Dreamtime sites many miles away.

Ethno. 1987.0c.4.7

Right **Oil Lamp**, Kumase, Ghana, c. 1980. H: 180 mm.
Left **Pair of gold-plated spectacles**, Baulé, Ivory Coast,
c. 1980. W: 140 mm.
Top **Electric light bulb decorated with beads**, Moru,
Sudan, c. 1980. H: 120 mm.

The reservoir of the lamp is made from an electric light
bulb. The other parts are cut from discarded tin cans. In
recent years electricity supplies have been increasingly
intermittent in the area of Ghana where this lamp was
made, and the object stands as an ironic comment on this
state of affairs. Modern costume jewellery like the gold
spectacles is now popular with chiefs in the Ivory Coast
and is a mark of prestige. The decorated bulb was made
in an area of Sudan which has no electricity; however,
the light bulb has provided a sympathetic armature upon
which the beadwork has been formed.

Ethno. 1983.Af5.31   Ethno. 1987.Af3.1   Ethno. 1979.Af6.10

Resist dyed *adire* cotton textile, Yoruba, Nigeria. 1900.
1.7 × 2.4 m.

This cloth has been painted freehand with starch before
dyeing in indigo, though it is copied from a stencilled
design. The figures in the central medallion are King
George V and Queen Mary and are doubtless copies from
Jubilee souvenirs of 1935.

Ethno. 1971.Af35.24

Opposite   **Composite wood figure/headdress.** Igbo,
Nigeria. c. 1920. H: 1.5 m. Presented by the Trustees of
the Wellcome Historical and Medical Museum.

These complex sculptures, incorporating animals and
human figures, act as the focal point for the dances of
particular masking societies. Each component is
separately carved and painted, then fitted onto a central
wooden armature.

Ethno. 1954.Af23.522

Model of a fish, Aswan town, Egypt. 1980s. L: 370 mm.
Presented by Ms Delia Pemberton.

These models, made of plastic sheeting and tinfoil biscuit
wrappers, are said to be amuletic charms hung in the
house to attract prosperity. The sharp scales of the fish
suggest that it may also have served to pierce the evil eye.

Ethno. 1989.Af1.1

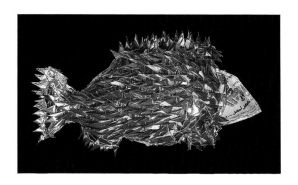

Dance bib, Acquired near Huancayo possibly Tarma, Junín, Peru, 1968. 810 × 490 mm.

Bib from horse costume depicting the military ruler and president Manuel Odria of the *ochenio* (8 years) in Peru (1948–56). The blue cloth bib with a hole for the neck and head is decorated with appliqué work of floral patterns and butterflies in different coloured threads, sequins, mirrors and glass. Odria is painted onto the cloth and is shown in a black velvet costume trimmed with gold braid, wearing the presidential band, and occupies the centre of the piece below the neck hole. The piece is inscribed DON MANUEL ODRIA in red sequins. Probably manufactured for a dance or event commemorating the visit of the president to the region.

Ethno. 1981.Am3.26

Feathered headdress, Mato Grosso or Pará, Brazil, collected in the 1980s. L: 2.5 m.

Triangular-shaped headdress manufactured from the long blue and red tail feathers of the papagaio or macaw. These feathers are knotted onto a base cord; at the tip of each is a white egret (?) feather. Featherwork, one of the major artistic contributions of the peoples of the Amazon, is usually manufactured and used by men on ceremonial occasions.

Ethno. 1986.Am17.4

marginal communities can survive and adapt in spite of partial integration into a notoriously fickle world economy. Since the seventeenth century, with the advent of trading companies exporting manufactured textiles to North America and Asia, the importation of cheap goods has often contributed to the destruction of local skills and indigenous markets. On the one hand modern imported goods may be used in an everyday setting, while on the other traditional objects may still be required for ritually significant events. Within this context, trade and exchange attitudes are inverted. What are utilitarian objects to a Westerner may be prized in other cultures – when transformed by local ingenuity – principally for their aesthetic value. In the same way, the West imports goods from other peoples and in certain circumstances categorises them as 'art'.

In collecting twentieth-century ethnography the role of tourist arts has been an increasingly important catalyst. Tourism can create new markets for goods, including new categories of products which can be of variable artistic quality and which may or may not incorporate ancient skills. It has often been criticised, with reason, for degrading the host culture. However, the demands of the tourist may also act to preserve local artistic skills, and indeed to develop them, sometimes leading to the creation of new traditions of considerable power. The arrival of new media, such as paper and printing in the Canadian Arctic, can give rise to what may seem superficially to be an urbanised Western product. But, in that particular case, Inuit comprehension of the environment, combined with a consummate sense of space and line, has created a fine art tradition which now, in a sense, symbolises Inuit society. Similarly, contemporary Australian Aboriginal artists have transferred ancient ideas of spirituality to canvas using acrylic paints. Elsewhere, but particularly in Asia, pre-existing traditions of two-dimensional artistic expression have combined with imported images and materials to produce syncretic schools of painting catering entirely to commercial needs – such as the decoration of rickshaws. Different forms of sculptural traditons have been adapted in equivalent, but rather different, ways. In West Africa

Sarape, Saltillo, Coahuila or Zacatecas, Mexico, early twentieth century. W: 1.12 m. L: 2.39 m

Tapestry woven in wool, aniline-dyed cotton and possibly silk, depicting George Washington. There is no known event mentioned or reason given for its manufacture. It was possibly made for sale at the market town of Taos, New Mexico. Some portrait sarapes of this type were woven in Zacatecas and were referred to as *Gobelinos* after the figurative work in French tapestries. Ethno. 1983.Am19.6

SAULO MORENO, **Wire skeleton figures**, Mexico City, Mexico, 1980s. H: 350 mm. L: 150 mm. W: 185 mm.

Painted papier-mâché and wire skeleton, with halo, fighting with a devil-dragon. In popular culture death and the devil are shown together and are linked to the major festival held during the first and second of November known as the Day of the Dead (All Souls Day).
Ethno. 1984.Am12.536

RICHARD GLAZER-DANAY (b. 1942), **Mohawk Lunch Pail.** Mohawk, Québec and New York c. 1980. L: 340 mm. Presented by the artist.

The Mohawk of Caughnawaga, Québec, are famous ironworkers responsible for the construction of numerous high-rise structures in eastern North America. This work was created as a comment on Mohawk sensibilities in the late twentieth century. In the artist's words, 'Most Mohawks drink Labatts beer but I like Moosehead better. If anyone asks about the pink buffs you can tell them that, while white people see pink elephants when drinking, Indians see pink buffalos. The nude backsides are a reference to ironworkers girl-watching at lunchtime.'
Ethno. 1983.Am37.1

PARR (1893–1969), **Harpooning Walrus**, Engraving, 1963. Inuit, Cape Dorset, Canada. 250 × 300 mm.

In the 1950s the Canadian federal government made available substantial assistance to Arctic communities to enable Inuit to create new art traditions. These Inuit artists drew on ancient perceptions of hunting, on an unequalled appreciation of their environment, and on their own exceptional aesthetic sense and manual dexterity. In the period from 1961 until his death, Parr created 32 prints, in editions of 50, which were sold in North America and Europe.

Ethno library

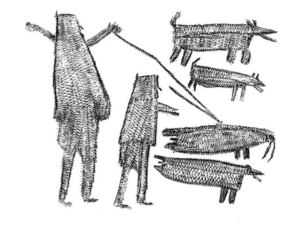

JESSIE WEBSTER (b. 1909), **Twined hat**, decorated with scenes of whaling, Ahousaht, British Columbia. 1981. H: 260 mm.

During the 1980s approximately 100 basketmakers wove twined basketry, both for native use and for sale, on Vancouver Island. Jessie Webster was one of the most skilled of these artists, specialising in making superb hats which were used as symbols of authority by leaders involved in political negotiations, and which were also sold to museums and private collectors.

Ethno. 1981.Am25.82

Painted panel for a rickshaw, Dhaka, Bangladesh. c. 1987.
Oil on tinplate, 660 × 250 mm.

Urban fantasy is a common theme in local popular painting. Modernity is
exaggerated by showing a skyline dominated by tall buildings, omitting rickshaws
and pedestrians, and by stretching cars and making bus travel look comfortable.
A minaret asserts the compatability of Islam and high technology. The reverse of
the tinplate shows that it is recycled from a soft-drink packaging company in
Atlanta.

Ethno. 1987.As16.17

Painted panel for a rickshaw, Dhaka, Bangladesh. c. 1987.
Oil on tinplate, 660 × 250 mm.

In this suburban rather than downtown scene, the emphasis is unusually on a
graceful, but still fantasized, form of traditional city life. It is as much a portrait of
the ornately-decorated rickshaw as of the neatly-dressed and comparatively well-fed
puller himself. By eulogizing the rickshaw as an appropriate means of transport, the
artist also pays tribute to his own means of livelihood.

Ethno. 1987.As16.15

the creation of masks and ritual paraphernalia, for use in celebrations commemorating ancestors and rites of passage, lead naturally in this century to the production of masks and other traditional sculpture for sale. This development is comparable to the tourist traditions created in the last decades in riverine and coastal Papua New Guinea. On the other hand, in East and Central Africa new traditions of the naturalistic representation of people and animals have emerged where previously such representational imagery was rare. In form, and in their role in the market place, these developments relate more closely to Inuit sculpture, for instance, than to the West African models or replicas of 'traditional' objects made for collectors and tourists.

The changing artistic and tourist traditions play a role, as the globalisation of culture intensifies, in satisfying the need for new or reconstituted national identities.

Collections act as an ever-expanding data base, not merely for scholars and anthropologists, but for people involved in a whole range of educational and artistic purposes. These include schools and universities as well as colleges of art and design. The provision of information about non-Western aesthetics and techniques, not just for designers and artists but for all visitors, is a growing responsibility for a Department whose own context is an increasingly multicultural European society.

J. C. H. King

Batik-dyed textile from Java, early twentieth century. L: 1.9 m.

Imported, machine-produced cotton was locally printed using metal templates. The borders are dyed red and feature popular motifs of birds, animals and plants. The large, indigo-dyed centre panel is adorned with repeated images taken from Dutch colonial life: gramophones, bicycles, parasols, fans and anchors, interspersed with the Star and Crescent of Islam, the local religion.

Ethno. 1934.3–7.70

Oriental Antiquities

ANON, **Pair of Doorgods**. Woodcuts made at Wu Qiang, Hebei province, late 1980s, c. 465 × 270 mm.

The tradition of popular prints produced for the Chinese New Year, and formerly also in the autumn, began at least as early as the Song dynasty (960–1279 AD), portraying folk gods and a range of narrative and auspicious themes.

OA 1991.2–13.06

Collections of Chinese and Japanese material entered the museum at its foundation in 1753, although the real impetus to develop this area did not come until late in the nineteenth century under the keepership of A W Franks. The present department emerged in 1921 when material was united from the departments of British and Medieval Antiquities and Ethnography, to be followed in 1933 by the Oriental prints and paintings formerly under the aegis of the Department of Prints and Drawings. With the exception of Japan, which has now been separated from the main collection, the department is concerned with the whole of Asia from the neolithic period to the present day; in the Middle East and North Africa its responsibilities start with the founding of Islam. The department is, in general, preoccupied by the growth of the major historical cultures and

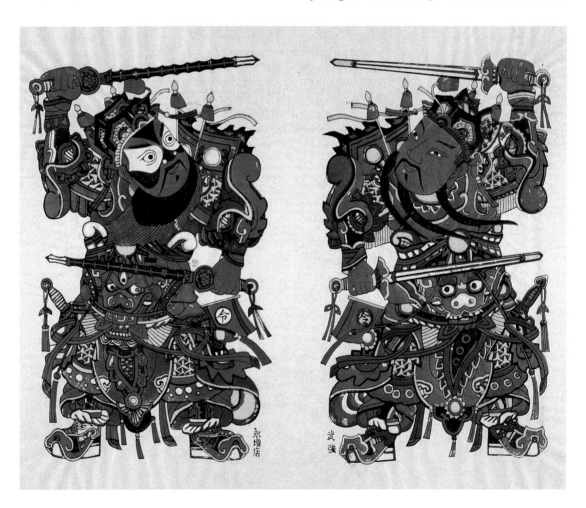

XIONG HAI (Cantonese:
Hung Hoi) (b. 1957),
Spring Landscape, 1988.
Hanging scroll, ink and
colours on paper,
645 × 899 mm.

Xiong Hai was born in
Xiamen, Fujian province.
He combines colour with
ink wash and dry
brushwork, achieving a
richness of texture and
depth of composition.

OA 1991.2–4.02 Add. 533

LI HONGREN (b. 1931), **Sun
Rising in the Eastern Sky**,
1984. Lithograph,
510 × 745 mm.

Li Hongren is an associate
professor and head of the
lithography section at the
Central Academy of Fine
Arts, Beijing. Although
lithography was first
introduced into China in
the nineteenth century, it
has only been taught in
art schools in China since
the 1950s.

OA 1987.12–24.07

Gu Yuan (b. 1919), **Burning of the Title Deeds**, 1947. Woodcut, 280 × 185 mm.

Gu Yuan was a former President of the Central Academy of Fine Arts, Beijing. He is one of the leading printmakers in the Modern Woodcut Movement initiated by Lu Xun (1881–1936) and inspired by the social-realist art of Germany and Russia.
OA 1987.12–24.05

Wang Qi (b. 1918), **The Rhythm of the Streets I**, 1985. Woodcut, 465 × 352 mm.

Wang Qi is now President of the Chinese Artists' Association and was a leading artist in the Modern Woodcut Movement. Despite the relaxation of the political restraints on art in the 1980s, many artists continued to portray conservative themes such as industry, urban life and cultural monuments.
OA 1987.12–24.019

their modern descendants, and is therefore principally concerned with complex urbanised societies.

Twentieth-century collecting is as much affected as that for earlier periods by the vast geographical scale and cultural diversity of the department's sphere of interest. The ancient civilizations of Asia were organised by means of religion and the written word, whose continuing importance is reflected in the department's emphasis on calligraphy, religious painting and other traditional painting styles. Another prin-

cipal area of collecting is in paper ephemera, including political posters, calendars, religious images, temple guides, festival stencils and paper cuts. The department's interest in paintings and prints executed in a more 'international style' is limited at present to a small-scale representation from each of the different regions through contacts with artists, and in the case of China, with the Central Academy of Fine Arts in Beijing. Works on paper account for the greater proportion of the twentieth-century acquisitions, but the range of activity has been extended to include some fine textiles, mainly from the Indian sub-continent so far, and high quality ceramics from Thailand, Korea and China to demonstrate recent artistic and technical achievements.

China and Korea

Outside Europe the Far East, led by China, was the only other part of the world to develop a self-conscious artistic tradition intended for the connoisseur, differing from the Islamic and Indian traditions which were primarily religious. Painting has continued throughout the twentieth century to occupy a dominant position in the hierarchy of artistic expression, as shown for example by the work of Fu Baoshi from the beginning of the century and the contemporary painter, Yang Yanping. Both artists evoke the character of their subjects, craggy cliffs and sodden lotus for example, through the interaction of brush, ink and paper. Their subjects are not, however, simply descriptive; mountains refer to notions of solitude and aspiration while the lotus is traditionally associated with purity amid the mire of worldly values.

The importance of painting and calligraphy within Chinese culture is such that the significance attached to the execution and ownership of original work extends to reproductions which enable a wider audience to share in the moral and aesthetic values of the past. Rubbings are made of calligraphy carved in stone tablets while sophisticated watercolour woodblock printing has been largely exploited as an adjunct to painting.

Printing was originally developed in China in the fifth or sixth centuries AD for the replication of Buddhist images; to this day it is still associated with religious ephemera and the work of comparatively humble artisans in contrast to the far more elevated status of painters and calligraphers. Prints by modern artists belong to a quite different lineage, stemming from a movement started by the writer, Lu Xun (1881–1936), in the late 1920s and 1930s, to create a new form of popular expression. Within this context woodblock printing was the natural choice of medium, drawing heavily upon the styles of Russian and German artists like Käthe Kollwitz, whose work had an explicitly social or political content. Other media which feature prominently in the prints of the last fifty years are traditional Chinese watercolour woodblock printing, and lithography, etching and silkscreening imported from the West. The socio-political slant has remained one

Jung Kwang (contemporary) **Riding the Tiger**, Korea, 1985. Lithograph, 750 × 550 mm.

The subject is a well-known one in Zen Buddhism. It refers to a Japanese Zen master, Takuan, who fearlessly jumped into the cage of a wild tiger sent from Korea to Japan in the early seventeenth century. The tiger's cage symbolises the situation of the Zen student.

OA 1991.7–23.01

Left **Porcelain lidded ewer** made by Mr Kim Cheekul, 1984.
H: 150 mm.
Right **Contemporary Korean vase** made by Mr Ahn Dong-oh, a master potter of porcelain.
H: 310 mm. Given by Sir David Wilson.

The ewer was made in a wood-fired kiln at Ichon, near Seoul. A distant reference back to the gourd- and melon-shaped celadon ewers of the Koryō dynasty is provided by the stalk-shaped knob on the lid. The pear-shaped porcelain vase is decorated with carved peony scrolls under a bluish-white *qingbai* type glaze.
OA 1990.11–14.4
OA 1986.3–15.1

YANG YANPING (b. 1934), **Autumn Lotus Pond**, 1985. Horizontal scroll, ink and colours on paper, 945 × 1760 mm.

Yang Yanping's work extends the tradition of Chinese ink painting (*guohua*) and pioneers techniques of brushless painting in which line drawing is often omitted.
OA 1987.5–27.01 Add. 514

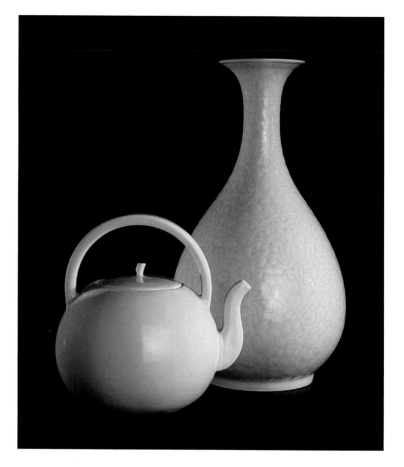

Chinese ceramics of the 1980s
Left **Stoneware teapot**, H: 124 mm. Addis Bequest.
Centre **Porcelain plate**, 220 mm. Addis Bequest.
Right **Greenware box and cover**, H: 105 mm.

The stoneware teapot in lotus form is an example of
Yixing ware, produced in east China from the sixteenth
century onwards, mainly for collectors. The porcelain
plate represents the current state of the underglaze
painted tradition established at Jingdezhen in south
China in the fourteenth century. The greenware box and
cover continues China's oldest and most illustrious
ceramic traditon.

OA 1984.2–2.99
OA 1984.2–2.58b
OA 1987.3–13.8

of the dominant features of Chinese printmaking,
whose subject matter has often been closely pres-
cribed by successive governments. Modernism
has been officially encouraged insofar as it is
appropriate to the portrayal of urban and
industrial advancement, which is often rendered
in a highly aesthetic manner rather startling to
Western conventions for imagery of this kind.
Since the Cultural Revolution a greater variety
of subject matter has been permissible, although
the previously-favoured themes of agriculture,
industry, urban life and cultural monuments
continue to be popular.

One of the most exciting recent developments

JANGADH SINGH SHYAM (b. 1962), **Untitled photogravure of a jungle scene**, Bhopal, Madhya Pradesh. Signed in *devanagari*. 1980s. Plate size 690 × 395 mm.

The work of this artist demonstrates a transition from a tribal, rural milieu to that of an urban one. Subject matter and its presentation are still drawn from the rich reservoir of tribal life, while technically the use of paper (rather than the wall of a house), and the use of photogravure are elements derived from traditions of urban and westernised society. A noticeable feature of such artists is the skill and humour with which they portray the animal and vegetable kingdoms. The position, and interest, of man is considered secondary.

OA 1988.2–9.09

Sahnji stencil used in the worship of Krishna. Mathura, Uttar Pradesh. 1980s. 357 × 282 mm.

Mathura, south of Delhi, is today the most important centre of Krishna worship and pilgrimage in India. At certain festivals hand-cut stencils are used in temples to prepare elaborate designs in coloured powders illustrating the life and rituals of Krishna. The one illustrated here is from a set of musicians and dancers associated with the festival of Holi.

OA 1989.2–4.033(64)

Manasa-pata from Bishnupur, Bankura, West Bengal. 1980s. Painted and varnished canvas, 830 × 670 mm.

Paintings such as this are used in the worship (*puja*) of the popular eastern Indian goddess, Manasa. She is particularly propitiated in connection with snakes and snake-bites, and is represented in sculpture from at least the eleventh century. Her depiction in this painting continues stylistic traditions found in nineteenth century clay sculpture and scroll-paintings.

OA 1989.2–4.058.

PAMPA PAUL, **The Greedy Cat**, 1988. Linocut print 3/9. Signed. Size of plate 410 × 330 mm.

Pampa Paul was a student in the Fine Arts Department at the MS. University at Baroda when this print was produced. The bright colouring perhaps reflects the influence of teachers at this prestigious school, such as Ghulam Mohammed Sheikh. The subject matter – fish and its consumption – would bring a wry smile to anyone noticing the name of the artist, for Bengalis are renowned for the lengths to which they will go in pursuit of good fresh fish.

OA 1989.2–4.021.

is the museum's work on Korea. The collection is being expanded in all areas, including contemporary ceramics and graphics. The unorthodox work of the Buddhist monk, Jung Kwang, for example, combines the spontaneity and directness of the Zen tradition with the boldness of traditional folk painting.

South Asia

While individual artistic personalities dominate the Islamic and Far Eastern collections, those from the Indian subcontinent and South-East Asia consist in the main of anonymous work produced, according to ancient religious traditions, by families of craftsmen and artists engaged in the service of temples and shrines. The Department has initiated and followed through a policy of collecting in India by region, assembling religious images and printed ephemera from different temples. A temple hanging from southern India, a painting of the deity Ganesha from Puri and Tibetan *thang-kas* relating the lives of famous lamas, are examples that stem from well-established lineages.

Popular religious tradition is represented by pilgrimage prints, mass-produced by photomechanical means, that are often displayed in domestic shrines. Examples of religious art from remote communities of India are also included which demonstrate the wide regional variation in interpretation of a common vocabulary. The need for economic survival has in itself often prompted new forms of expression among rural societies; apotropaic traditions of painting which originated in the house paintings of groups such as the Worli and Saora of Central India are now painted on paper in order to find currency in a wider market.

Despite the strength of religious traditions, artistic production and imagery are becoming more secularised; even artists from families dedicated exclusively to religious work are now executing material, which though it is recognisably Indian to Western eyes, represents a complete break with accepted subject matter. A case in point is the textile painting by Deshbandu Mahapatra showing the trees of Orissa as recorded in the manuscript collections of the state library at Bhuvaneshvar.

Thang-ka illustrating the life of Sönam Lo-trö (bSod-nams Blo-gros), Lama 'Merit Intellect'. Dolpo, Nepal. 1960/61. 1.03 × 0.8 m. (framed).
Given by Professor David L Snellgrove, in appreciation of Pasang Khambache Sherpa, the faithful companion of his Himalayan travels, 1953–1979.

One of a series of four, this *thang-ka* illustrates the text now translated by the donor and published as *Four Lamas of Dolpo*. It depicts, in comic-strip fashion, the events of the life of the Abbot of Margom (dMar-sgom), who lived between 1456 and 1521; he is shown centrally. The artist is unknown, other than that he was a lama of the 'Residence of Great Happiness' at Namdo, in the Kang-khong valley of Dolpo, in northwestern Nepal.
OA 1989.11–6.01

Sarangpur's Hanuman. Photomechanical print signed by Deepak, and printed in Surat, Gujarat. 1980s.
497 × 350 mm.

This colourful religious print is an example of a common type seen throughout South and Southeast Asia. Sold primarily at the temple to which they relate – here Sarangpur – they are purchased by pilgrims for use in domestic shrines. Hanuman, the lieutenant of Rama, figures prominently in the epic, the Ramayana, though rarely enjoys his own temple cult. Where he does, as at Sarangpur, it is perhaps the result of a conflation of a tribal animal cult, and a high caste Hindu cult. Here this interpretation is borne out by the lack of iconographical features which relate to the epic.
OA 1988.2–9.045(38)

Opposite Deshbandu Mahapatra. **Patachitra** (painted textile scroll) of tussar silk. 1980s. It illustrates the trees of the eastern Indian state of Orissa as recorded in manuscripts now in the State Library, in Bhuvaneshvar (the capital of Orissa). 2.36 × 1.185 m.

This commissioned work illustrates the way in which the traditions of some Indian painting schools have been revivified through the opening up of new, urban markets. Coastal Orissa, especially the districts close to the pilgrimage town of Puri, has been the centre of a major religious painting tradition. This *patachitra* is in that same Orissa style, but the subject matter is secular and suitable for domestic decorative use. The trees, drawn from examples in manuscripts, vary from the naturalistic to the stylised.
OA 1989.2–4.070.

DIA AL-AZZAWI (b. Baghdad 1939), **Adonis**, 1990. Lithograph 1/6, 1100 × 385 mm.

From an edition of five hand-coloured lithographs illustrating the poems of the Lebanese poet Adonis, produced on the occasion of his sixtieth birthday. The poem transcribed and illustrated here is 'This is my name', written in 1968.

OA 1990.11–23.01

Other artists, usually working in urban contexts, have been more exposed to international cultural trends. Art schools, which have been part of the Indian educational system since the last century, now assume a much greater importance; the most renowned today are those at Baroda and Shantiniketan, with reciprocal programmes linking them with institutions abroad such as the Royal College of Art in London. New printmaking techniques like lithography and intaglio methods have been introduced but, despite their international contacts, many artists trained in the art schools continue to derive their chief inspiration from the immense variety found in Indian traditions. These include the abstract designs of religious diagrams, the visual and symbolic power of the written word and the emotional response to the imposing antiquity and grandeur of the landscape.

Islamic World

Islamic art as such was really a court art which came to an end in the mid-nineteenth century. Thereafter the work produced from the Islamic world has been very much conditioned by national divisions but although it can no longer be given a generic name, many of the artists represented, whether Iraqi, Algerian, Lebanese or Iranian, show a continuing interest in that aspect of their visual culture which binds Muslims together, Arabic writing. Among individual artists there are striking differences of approach. Ahmed Mustafa (whose work is displayed in the Addis Gallery) and Hossein Zenderoudi are traditionalists using verses from

RACHID KORAICHI (b. Algeria 1947), **Poèmes sur an amour ancien**, 1980s. Lithograph 8/12. 700 × 500 mm.

This work is inspired by a poem bearing the same title by Palestinian poet Mahmud Darwish. Phrases from the poem are transcribed, with talismanic designs on two sides. In the centre is an imaginary Japanese character reminiscent of the character 'mau', to dance.

OA 1990.10–10.01

NJA MAHDAOUI (b. Tunisia 1937), **Untitled**, 1980s. Ink on parchment, 1 × 1 m.

Mahdaoui uses the shapes of Arabic letters, removing meaning and simply delighting in the Kufic and cursive forms themselves.

OA 1991.6–6.02

the Koran with brilliant proficiency of execution and boldness of colour. The Algerian painter, Rachid Koraichi, is interested in the secret meaning of Arabic letters; around the sides of 'Poèmes sur un amour ancien' are magic squares with individual numbers and letters which were traditionally used as talismans. A more dramatic departure from accepted calligraphic conventions is the work of the Tunisian artist, Nja Mahdaoui, whose large compositions, often done on parchment, are devoid of textual meaning, simply revelling in the formal shapes associated with Kufic script.

The most important of the artists represented in the collection is the Iraqi painter, Dia al-Azzawi. Although he sometimes uses writing as part of his compositions, his work is not allied to the calligraphic tradition. The series of hand-tinted lithographs, which was produced on the occasion of the sixtieth birthday of the Lebanese poet Adonis, exemplifies al-Azzawi's vivid use of colour combined with both Western figurative images and a more purely Islamic interest in abstract line.

Jessica Rawson

Japanese Antiquities

The Japanese material acquired during the early part of the museum's history, in common with that from the other Oriental cultures, was collected as 'curiosities' rather than as historic documents or works of art and craftsmanship. This attitude prevailed until the 1860s, when the interest in *Japonisme* spread to Britain from the Continent. Thereafter, more serious efforts were made to collect older Japanese material, first ceramics, metalwork, lacquer and sculpture, then painting, and finally in the 1890s woodblock prints and illustrated books. Throughout the twentieth century these continued to be vigorously acquired within the context of what came to be the Department of Oriental Antiquities, but it was only in 1960 that a Japan specialist was first appointed.

Japanese studies and collecting developed fast and in 1980 the first formal steps were taken to build up a systematic collection of twentieth-century prints based on the strength of the museum's existing holding of graphic art executed prior to 1910. The collection now comprises about 2,500 prints, portfolios and illustrated books, covering all major schools and almost all important artists to the present day. Such rapid progress has been greatly facilitated by the acquisition of three collections made in Japan by enthusiastic foreign collectors, Robert Vergez, Gaston Petit and Scott Johnson. This initiative was part of a growing perception that Japan's twentieth-century artistic achievements merited a proper representation in the British Museum, one of the factors in the creation of a separate Department of Japanese Antiquities in 1987. The main impetus for this development came from the work involved in the fundraising, planning and construction for the new Japanese Galleries which opened in April 1990. These galleries provide a further incentive to collecting in the contemporary field, for they are seen by Japanese artists and craftsmen as a prestigious showcase; already they are generating displays of twentieth-century materials and a succession of important gifts to the collections. Donations have indeed proved to be the best source of contemporary painting in traditional styles and formats, and of calligraphy. Both these major arts command such high prices in Japan itself, that

UJIHARU NAGASAWA (contemporary), **Mask of *Okina***. Painted wood with human hair, 183 mm. Given by Mr Nohzin Suzuki.

This is the oldest type of mask used in the classical *Nō* drama; it is restricted to the ancient dance/drama *Okina* ('The old man') and is more Shinto in feeling than the dominant Buddhist sentiment of *Nō*.

JA 1986.11.3.2

SEKKA KAMIZAKA (1866–1942), 'White Heron'
(*Shirasagi*) from Volume I of *Momoyogusa* ('Grasses of a
myriad worlds'), 1910. Woodblock, published by Unsōdō
of Kyoto, opening 300 × 445 mm.

The three volumes of *Momoyogusa* are one of the greatest
achievements of Japanese design and of the woodblock
print. In this composition, a white heron is seen by a
wicker basket which was filled with stones to protect
river banks from erosion (*jakago*).
JA SJ 161

SHIKŌ MUNAKATA (1900–75), Hawk Woman (*Taka
Onna*), 1955. Woodblock with hand-colouring, size of
sheet approx 540 × 415 mm.

One of Munakata's most powerful designs, this was first
exhibited in Tokyo in 1956. The hand-colouring, as in
many of his post-war works, is applied both on the front
and the back of the thin hand-made paper. Munakata's
primitive energy and extraordinarily instinctive and free
block-cutting (often done without reference to drawings)
made him the most effective of all Japan's print-artists
this century and the one with by far the biggest
international reputation.
JA 1987,3–16.0430

Un'ichi Hiratsuka (b. 1895), *Fūkugawa Kiba* (**The woodyards at Fukagawa**), one print from a series of twelve entitled 'Tokyo after the Earthquake' (*Tōkyō Shinzaiseki Fūkei*) 1925. Woodblock 23/50, published by Hisayoshi Yamaguchi. Size of sheet approx 275 × 354 mm.

This series is one of the monuments of the Creative Print Movement (*Sōsaku Hanga*), and one of the few works of art to record unflinchingly the horror of the 1923 earthquake and fire, Japan's greatest peacetime disaster. This was also one of the destabilizing events which led to the rise of Japan's fascist regime, of which the *Sōsaku Hanga* artists were generally opponents.

JA 1987.10.14.012

Kōshirō Onchi (1889–1955), **Form No 7. Grotesque I ('B' Impression)**, 1948. Woodblock, size of sheet 550 × 430 mm.

One aspect of Onchi's work was always abstract, and it came to a splendid late flowering in his last ten years. In prints such as this his powers as a colourist are very evident. The 'A' impression of this print (Juda Collection, Los Angeles) is rather lighter-toned in the reds.

JA 1989.3-14.077

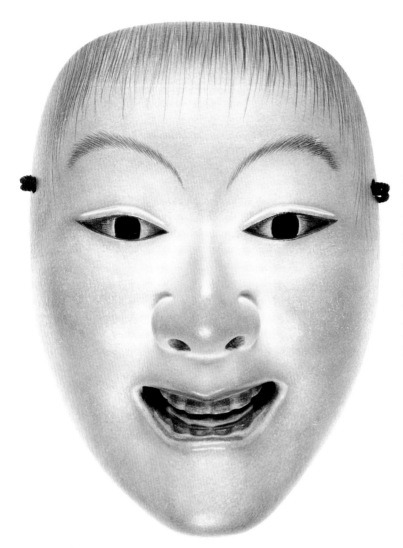

Noнzin Suzuki (contemporary), **Mask of Shitadashi-Dōji**. Painted wood, 195 mm. Given by the maker, Mr Nohzin Suzuki.

Masks are worn by the two principal characters in *Nō* dramas, and sometimes by others if not human beings. The 'Boy with Tongue Sticking Out' is a semi-human drunken creature with a red face and disheveled hair. Suzuki is one of the leading contemporary carvers of *Nō* masks.
JA 1986.11.3.1

they would otherwise be beyond the British Museum's means.

Despite the extent to which Japan has become a modern, industrialised society, it has preserved its most important cultural and artistic traditions with great tenacity. Unlike the other East Asian nations which have had a Western technology and way of life imposed upon them through political and economic domination, Japan, until the end of the Pacific War, was able to control the degree of foreign influence. This facilitated the integration of certain aspects of modernisation without threatening the Japanese sense of their own cultural identity. A favourable climate existed for the revival of traditional painting

(*Nihonga*) which was at its peak in the years 1900–1940, the Creative Print Movement (*Sōsaku Hanga*) at its most vigorous from 1915–1975, and the Folk Art Movement (*Mingei*) first formally proposed by Sōetsu Yanagi in 1926.

With the Allied Occupation from 1945 to 1952, a completely new era began. The rate of change was rapidly accelerated with considerable consequences for artistic production. A more Americanised educational system led to a proliferation of colleges of higher education which supplanted the prolonged apprenticeship training for artists, with a concomitant increase in the number of artists working both at home and abroad. While post-war developments have introduced a far greater internationalism to Japanese artistic expression, they have also helped to foster indigenous skills. The lifting of restrictions after years of nationalist censorship created a much freer artistic climate conducive to the flowering of the talent of the finest exponent of the Creative Print Movement from 1945–1955, Kōshirō Onchi. The intense admiration of many foreigners for the arts of Japan has promoted revivals of traditional skills in certain areas, most notably that of netsuke-carving since the 1960s. There are now scores of carvers of these miniature toggles who sell principally to the West. Few connoisseurs would contest the view that they are as good, if not better, than those of the eighteenth and nineteenth centuries. The British Museum has a small collection of these and related small-scale carvings which it expects to enhance further through a comprehensive exhibition in 1993. By then the carvers will almost all be working in wood since ivory can no longer be imported, and will thus revert to the traditional bias of the Japanese themselves for wooden sculpture. Mask-carving, in which the collection is also being extended by donation, has by contrast always been done in wood; the continuing vitality of the classic Nō drama and of Kagura (local Shinto folk-dancing and drama) have ensured its survival as a specialised art.

The abiding prestige of the traditions of the Tea Ceremony continue to promote the arts of pottery, flower-arrangement and calligraphy, while the preference of most Japanese for the old style of interior furnishing based on *tatami* flooring units has perpetuated a way of eating and drinking which stimulates new and varied styles of ceramics and lacquer tablewares. The strength of demand for these goods has engendered a solid financial background against which distinguished art potters and decorators can continue to produce work of the very highest quality. In recognition of the importance of their achievement, the museum has just decided to extend its holding of porcelains up to the present day through deliberate purchase as well as through acceptance of gifts, building on the splendid coverage already existing as far as 1900.

Lawrence Smith

Isshū Kishi (b. 1917), **Netsuke carved as a group of masks**. Ivory, 48 mm.

The masks are from the *Nō* and *Kyōgen* dramas, and are intended as a miniature tour-de-force of the carver's art. The maker is usually known by his art-name Isshū.
JA 1981.10.14.2

Bishū Saitō (b. 1943), **Netsuke in the shape of a long-tailed fox with a bird-feather**. Ivory, 47 mm.

The long-tailed fox is one of the many mythical forms of an animal which constantly appears in Japanese folk-stories, almost always in an unfavourable light. This is a classic, rounded form of the *netsuke* (retaining toggle), the openwork structure allowing a cord to be tied to it. The maker is usually known by his art-name Bishū.
JA 1981.10.14.1

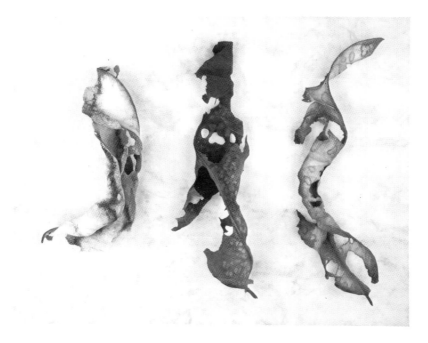

KŌDŌ OKUDA (b. 1940), **Three 'Withered Leaves' (*Kareha*)**. Tinted ivory, 153 mm. 185 mm. 221mm. Given by the maker, Mr Kōdō Okuda.

Okuda was originally a carver of *netsuke* (traditional retaining toggles), and an ink-painter, but later turned to an ambitious series of models of fallen leaves, each one based on a real leaf and taking several months to complete. The series will end when he has used up the stock of ivory inherited from his father, also an ivory carver.

JA 1986.1.30.1–3

NOBORU SŌMA (contemporary), **'White Celadon' porcelain bowl with relief vortex decoration**. H: 210 mm. Bought with the help of a donation from Sir David Wilson.

Sōma is one of the younger members of the large colony of potters working today in Ibaragi Prefecture, to the north of Tokyo. A superb technician on the wheel, he also specialises in the very pale greenish glaze known as 'white celadon' (*haku seiji*), while on some pieces his wife decorates in traditional underglaze blue.

JA 1991.4.15.1

Medieval and Later Antiquities

Glass vase, with a mould-blown bowl set on a pressed glass base. Designed by Chris Lebeau (1878–1945) in 1924–5 and made by the Glasfabriek Leerdam in Holland. H: 275 mm.

Lebeau was one of a number of outside artists commissioned to design glass for Leerdam in the 1920s. His startling colour combinations and highly original shapes were unlike anything else produced at the time either in Holland or elsewhere.

MLA 1988,7–11,1

The broadly-defined title of this department reflects its evolution through successive sub-divisions of the original Department of Antiquities, until it assumed its present form in 1969. A W Franks, who joined the Museum in 1851, was the dominant force in the development of the Renaissance and later collections. With his astonishing range of acquisitions for the department during his lifetime, and the bequest of his own collection of ceramics, silver, finger-rings etc in 1897, Franks did much to bridge the gap between the past and the present. It was he, too, who helped to define the British Museum's sense of historical and documentary purpose as being an equally important guiding principle for the acquisition of post-Medieval material as it was for earlier antiquities.[1]

The museum's acquisitions of contemporary material during the nineteenth and early twentieth centuries were mainly gifts or bequests and so formed a haphazard collection, but one that contained a number of interesting items on which more recent acquisitions have built. The collection of Felix Slade, bequeathed to the museum in 1868 and celebrated for its outstanding Roman and Venetian glass, included two contemporary pieces purchased at international exhibitions. One of these was an engraved glass tazza made by the Cristalleries de Clichy, France, shown at the International Exhibition in London in 1862. The catalogue of the Slade collection, published in 1871, notes that this tazza 'was selected as one of the best examples of engraved glass at the Exhibition, and this must be the excuse for introducing so modern a specimen into this catalogue.'

The twentieth century opened with the acquisition of a spectacular piece of Sèvres porcelain, a huge vase decorated in *pâte-sur-pâte* by Taxile Doat in 1895 and presented by the French government in March 1901 in return for thirty thousand pamphlets on the French Revolution, which the British Museum had presented to the Bibliothéque Nationale and the Municipal Library of Paris. In July 1902, Bernard Moore presented six ceramic pieces described in the acquisitions register as 'the first results of attempts to produce Chinese flambé on porcelain'; they are the earliest securely datable

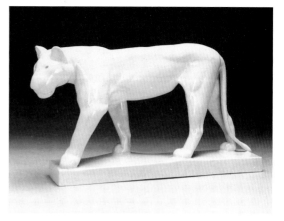

Porcelain figure of a lioness, designed by the sculptor Gerhard Marcks (1889–1974) in 1909–10 and made by the Schwarzburger Werkstätten für Porzellankunst, Thuringia, Germany. L: 440 mm.

The lioness is part of a group of three animal figures owned by the British Museum, the others being a falcon and a lynx. These are Marcks' earliest sculptural works and represent an attempt to produce traditional porcelain figures in a more modern idiom. Marcks later directed the pottery workshop at the Bauhaus.
MLA 1990,4–6,3

Glass tazza, designed by Harry Powell (1853–1922), and made by James Powell & Sons, Whitefriars Glass Works, London, in 1902.
H: 210 mm.

Harry Powell was director of the family firm of Powell & Sons. This pale green tazza, with its engraved and applied decoration of gannets and waves, was made for display at the international exhibition at Turin in 1902, and is one of the finest examples of English Art Nouveau glass.

MLA 1988,4–2,1

Glass vase, designed in 1921 by Vittorio Zecchin (1878–1947) for the newly-founded firm of Cappelin-Venini in Murano, Italy. H: 221 mm.

Zecchin's purist shapes in pastel colours (this vase is pale green) broke away from traditional, highly-decorated Venetian glass and demonstrated the influence of glass design in other European countries. The shape was known as 'Veronese' because it was inspired by a vase depicted in a painting of the Annunciation by the sixteenth-century artist Paolo Veronese.
MLA 1991,1–8,1

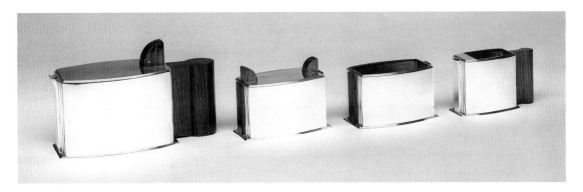

Silver teaset, designed in 1929 and made in the workshops of Jean Puiforcat, Paris. H of teapot: 130 mm. Given by Mr and Mrs John Cox.

Puiforcat was the leading designer of modernist silver in France after the First World War and inspired much of the work of his contemporaries.

MLA 1981,3–11,2–5

Oak clock with stencilled decoration, designed by the architect Charles Rennie Mackintosh (1868–1928) in 1919 for the house of the engineering-model manufacturer, W J Bassett-Lowke, in Northampton. H: 370 mm.

The clock was intended to fit into Mackintosh's boldly redesigned interior with its striking geometric wallpaper and matching furniture and fittings.

MLA 1980,5–19,1

examples of his *flambé* and other lustrous glazes, and were inspired by his familiarity with the British Museum collection and his friendship with its keeper, R L Hobson. Another fine piece of lustre pottery is the dish decorated by William De Morgan in 1880 and bequeathed by his associate, Halsey Ricardo, in 1928. In 1945 the museum received a bequest of Martinware from Ernest Marsh, who had bought much of his collection from the Martin Brothers themselves between 1887 and 1915, and in 1969 Peter Wilding bequeathed his collection of Cartier cigarette boxes.

The horological collections have been built up from a variety of sources, and include many fine decorative pieces, but the emphasis is on the representation of technical improvement in the development of watch and clock movements up to the present day. The bequests of Lady Fellowes in 1874 and of Octavius Morgan in 1888 concentrated on historical material. It was not until 1958, with the acquisition of the collection of C A Ilbert, that the collections were extended to modern times. They have since been kept up to date; recent acquisitions have included twentieth-century watches from the Ingersoll factory archive and a unique technical masterpiece made in 1976 by the pre-eminent contemporary watchmaker, George Daniels.

The arrival in 1978 of the Hull Grundy Gift of jewellery transformed the collections in many ways; in particular it brought the British Museum's collections of jewellery into the twentieth century, with its distinguished Art Nouveau pieces by Lalique, Boucheron, Feuillâtre and others. Professor and Mrs Hull Grundy also gave some twenty pieces of Martinware to add to the

Silver tea-infuser, designed by Marianne Brandt (1893–1983) in 1924 at the Bauhaus, Weimar. H: 73 mm.

The Bauhaus emphasised form rather than decoration, and aimed to produce designs suitable for industrial production. This tea-infuser is now famous as a classic Bauhaus object, but is in fact handmade and thus remains in the tradition of costly craft-based metalworking.
MLA 1979,11–2,1

Art Nouveau ceramics and metalwork, late 1890s to 1902.

Left to right: **vase with sang-de-boeuf** glaze, Henry van de Velde, 1902; **vase**, Peter Behrens, 1901; **tall vase**, Artus van Briggle, Colorado Springs, 1902; **copper vase** (H: 737 mm), Frank Lloyd Wright, late 1890s; **brass kettle**, Jan Eisenlöffel, Holland, 1902.

MLA 1986,11–2,1, MLA 1989,1–2,1, MLA 1984,7–3,2, MLA 1985,5–5,1, MLA 1987,1–10,1

Art Nouveau jewellery c. 1900–14. Many of these pieces were given by Professor and Mrs J Hull Grundy in 1978 (HG Gift).

Top: **Comb** by F Partridge, London. W: 105 mm. MLA HG Gift, cat. no. 1096; **Waist-clasp** of Copenhagen porcelain. L: 114 mm. MLA HG Gift, cat. no. 1115; *Centre*: **Comb** designed by H van de Velde. W: 79 mm. MLA 1980,6–15,1; **Carved horn** *plaque-de-cou* (W: 80 mm) and **hatpin** by R Lalique. MLA HG Gift, cat. nos. 1095, 1094; **Gold buckle** by Boucheron for the Paris Exhibition of 1900. H: 78 mm. MLA HG Gift, cat. no. 1113; *Below*: **Gold and enamel pendant** designed by E Colonna for S Bing's Maison de l'Art Nouveau, Paris. L: 88 mm. MLA 1991,7–11,1; **Silver brooch** designed by G Jensen, Copenhagen. W: 65 mm. MLA 1981,6–8,1; **Silver and enamel pendant** by the firm of T Fahrner, Pforzheim. W: 35 mm. MLA 1990,6–8,1

Porcelain plate with Suprematist decoration, designed by
I G Chashnik (1902–29) and painted at the State
Porcelain Factory, Petrograd in 1923. D: 237 mm.

The Suprematist movement was begun by Malevich
c. 1913–15; his most famous work shows a black square
on a white ground. The abstract shapes and pure colours
of Suprematism were adapted to porcelain by Malevich
and his pupils, among whom was Chashnik.
MLA 1988.6–9.2

Marsh bequest and a small group of silver.

As a consequence, in the following year the
Trustees decided that the collections should be
selectively, but actively, extended into the twentieth century. This was part of an overall British
Museum strategy, but the collecting criteria continued to place the same emphasis on documentary significance as had applied to earlier
material. Thus an effort has been made to acquire
pieces that are signed or dated, or have some
interesting historical association, so that they
represent the designers, manufacturers, schools
and movements that have contributed to the
development of the decorative arts in the twentieth century, in both avant-garde and traditional forms.

The decision to confine the new collections to
the field of ceramics, glass and metalwork was
a corollary of their purpose as an extension of the
existing collections. Similarly, the decision not to
pursue the collections at present much beyond

1950 follows from the desire to preserve their
historical character as well as a recognition of the
V&A's more comprehensive role in this area. In
due course the collections will be extended into
later years, but always after the lapse of some
decades. A special purchase fund of £15,000 was
allocated from the Trustees' central acquisitions
fund in the first year and now stands at £20,000
per annum. The Trustees have also contributed
additional sums from the central fund to purchase a number of outstanding individual items.

As presently constituted, the collections are
international in scope and range from indi-
vidually-made to mass-produced items. For
example, the collection of American material,
much of which is rare outside its country of
origin, includes one of Frank Lloyd Wright's
custom-built flower vases or 'weed-holders' as
well as mass-produced industrial ceramics
designed by Russel Wright in the late 1930s. The
collections are especially strong in Continental
Art Nouveau and in German material of the
period 1890–1940, including one of the few
surviving versions of Marianne Brandt's classic
silver tea-infuser designed at the Bauhaus in
1924, as well as more specialist aspects such as
early twentieth-century German stoneware
which continues the Museum's existing holdings
in this area. To complement the Hull Grundy Gift
and to illustrate an entirely different aspect of the
jewellery trade, the Department has recently
acquired a collection of documentary imitation
jewellery made on a large scale in Birmingham
in the period c. 1880–1920 and presented by the
manufacturers, N C Reading & Co.

Acquisition policy always pays due regard to
other national collections. Representation of the
English Arts and Crafts Movement and of Scandinavian ceramics has been deliberately restricted,
as the V&A has comprehensive collections in
these areas. Instead, there has been an attempt
to acquire material from Germany, Holland and
America. As yet there is little from Italy or
Czechoslovakia; it is hoped that lacunae such as
these will be filled in the future, and the scope
of the collection broadened in line with the archaeological traditions of the department.

Judy Rudoe

Glass coffee-percolator, designed by Gerhard Marcks (1889–1974) between 1925–30. Made by Schott Glaswerke, Jena, Germany, between 1930–39. Total H: 274 mm.

This is one of the first coffee machines in fireproof glass. Schott's fireproof glass was developed for scientific purposes and their early coffee machines were thought to look too much like laboratory ware. Marcks, who had directed the Bauhaus pottery workshop, was therefore asked to create a new model.

MLA 1981,12–3,1

Two sets of glasses made by the Libbey Glass Manufacturing Company, Toledo, Ohio, USA; the square-based tumblers designed by A D Nash in 1931–2, the service with columnar stems designed by W D Teague and E W Fuerst in 1939 for the State Dining Room in the Federal Building at the New York World's Fair. H of tumblers: 143 mm, 123 mm, 82 mm.
MLA 1988,6–8,5–7
H of tallest stemmed glass: 220 mm.
MLA 1988,6–8,1–4

Chromium-plated brass pitcher, designed by Peter Müller-Munk (1907–67) in 1935 and made by the Revere Brass and Copper Company, Rome, New York. H: 305 mm.

This pitcher was known as the 'Normandie' pitcher because its shape was blatantly derived from that of the front of the celebrated French ocean liner launched in 1935. Its streamlined construction is highly original; the body is formed of one sheet of metal bent to shape. Müller-Munk was a silversmith who came to America from Germany in 1926.

MLA 1988,11–3,1

**Group of 'American Modern' and 'Casual China'
dinnerware**, two different services designed by Russel
Wright (1904–76) in 1937 and 1946.
H: of pitcher: 267 mm.

'American Modern' became one of the most popular
mass-produced patterns for informal dinnerware ever
sold, and the standard present for young brides in the
early 1940s. Its success lay in its unprecedentedly
asymmetrical organic shapes and in its equally
unconventional colours. The butter dish and dark grey
carafe are 'Casual China'.

Pitcher and butter dish   MLA 1988,1–17,1 and 2

Plate and dark grey carafe. Given by David Kiehl.

MLA 1988,1–16,1;   MLA 1989,7–10,1

Celery dish and shakers   MLA 1988,1–18,1, 2a and b

Cream jug   MLA 1989,1–8,3

Gravy boat   MLA 1989,1–8,2 and 2a

Pale grey carafe   MLA 1989,1–8,1

GEORGE DANIELS (b. 1926), **Gold watch with silver dial
and gold hands, gold fob chain and key**, London, 1976.
D: 62 mm. Bequeathed by C. Clutton Esq.

The Department of Medieval and Later Antiquities has
responsibility for one of the world's finest horological
collections, containing some four thousand items. This
unique technical masterpiece has two going trains
driving a single balance over Daniels' independent
double-wheel escapement.

MLA 1991,4–5,1

References

1   See Timothy Wilson 'The origins of the Maiolica
Collections of the British Museum and the Victoria and
Albert Museum 1851–55' in *Faenza*, LXXI, no 1–3, 1985,
pp 68–94.

Prints and Drawings

CHARLES RENNIE MACKINTOSH (1868–1928), **Stylised Tulips**. Design for silk. Graphite and watercolour on tracing paper, 220 × 150 mm.

One of the many textile designs produced by Mackintosh after he moved to Chelsea in 1915. He worked on commission for the firms of Foxton's and Sefton's, receiving between £5 and £20 for each design. This particular example appears to have been priced at 10 guineas.

PD 1984–1–21–7

Geographically, the scope of the collection covers Europe and those societies culturally associated with it in other parts of the world, principally the United States, Canada, Latin America, Australia, New Zealand and Israel. The foundation of the department's twentieth-century collection was laid by the distinguished scholar Campbell Dodgson (1867–1948), who joined the staff in 1893 and acted as Keeper from 1912–1932. During his lifetime he made countless gifts himself and attracted many others by virtue of his position and reputation; at his death he bequeathed his personal collection of over 5,000 items. From the outset Dodgson conceived his collection as a complement to the existing holdings of the department, concentrating his purchases in the field of modern prints where the museum was weakest. His taste was avowedly conservative, eschewing the more avant-garde trends of the early twentieth century like Cubism and Expressionism. Nonetheless, Dodgson's range of interests was completely international, encompassing French, German, East European, Scandinavian and American material as well as British; he acquired important examples of the early etchings of Käthe Kollwitz, Emil Nolde, Carl Larsson, Edvard Munch and Edward Hopper and a notable group of Matisse's lithographs from the 1920s. Dodgson was also active in the Contemporary Art Society, founded in 1910, which maintained a separate fund for the purchase of prints and drawings from 1919 until 1945; the fund was administered by Dodgson and his successor, A M Hind, with about 75% of the acquisitions going to the British Museum. After the Second World War, although the department continued to benefit from the allocations made by the CAS, they did not amount to more than a very small number of items. The acquisition of twentieth-century material fell largely into abeyance until 1967 when the Trustees, together with the C G and S L Bernstein Trust, created a small fund of £2000 per annum specifically for the purchase of Modern Graphic art. Seven years later the Director at that time, Sir John Pope-Hennessy, established a curatorial post with responsibility for the collection from 1890 onwards while his successor, Sir David Wilson, reinforced the museum's commitment to this period by assign-

EDWARD HOPPER (1882–1967), **Night on the El Train** 1918. Etching, 185 × 200 mm.

Hopper, who became the greatest of all the American Realist painters this century, first found his own style and subject matter in the etchings and drypoints he made from 1915 to 1923. The department owns four of these prints, all presented by Campbell Dodgson, who purchased them for between $18 and $22.

PD 1926-6-24-15

ing in 1979 two separate funds of £25,000 each for the acquisition of modern prints and drawings; the drawings fund was subsequently doubled in 1985.

Despite the many lacunae arising from the fitful nature of the department's twentieth-century collecting activities, Campbell Dodgson's interests have provided an invaluable point of departure for the concerted efforts of the past fifteen years to establish coherent groups of material within the collection as a whole. The American, German and British schools have received particular attention, but the range of acquisition has been expanded to include areas which are poorly represented in public collections in this country: Canada, Mexico, Eastern Europe, Scandinavia and the Netherlands. The purchasing policy has been further enhanced by the British Museum Society's allocation in 1983 of a special fund for contemporary drawings by artists working in Britain; the presentation of a comprehensive collection of twentieth-century Czechoslovak prints in 1985 through an exchange with the National Gallery in Prague; then most recently of all, the Rausing Fund has been donated for the development of the Scandinavian collection. The acquisitions policy is determined first and foremost by the department's principal role as a reference collection and the extensive use made of its resources for teaching purposes; this enables the museum to embrace a far greater diversity of material than would be appropriate for an

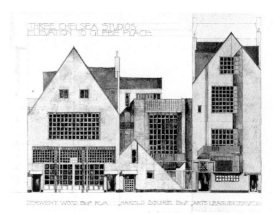

CHARLES RENNIE MACKINTOSH (1868–1928), **Three Chelsea Studios. Elevation to Glebe Place**, 1920 Graphite and watercolour, 280 × 378 mm.

Mackintosh received very few architectural commissions after he left Glasgow in 1914. This is one of three elevations in the British Museum for the same scheme, commissioned by three fellow-artists and the Arts League of Service. The high cost of the work involved, however, prevented the realisation of all but a modified version of the design for Harold Squire's studio.

PD 1981-12-12-22

OTTO DIX (1891–1969), **Lens is attacked with bombs**, 1924
Plate 33 from *Der Krieg*, portfolio of fifty etchings
numbered 31/70, 297 × 244 mm.

Dix was well aware of the precedent of Goya's 'Disasters
of War' in creating his own graphic cycle which became
the starkest of all visual statements about the First World
War.

PD 1982-7-24-28(33)

A R PENCK (b. 1939), **Dancing figure from *8 Erfahrungen***
(8 Experiences), 1981. Woodcut from the boxed set of 8,
numbered 13/50, 658 × 512 mm.

The work of A R Penck, a pseudonym for Ralf Winkler,
has been deeply affected by his experiences as a dissident
within East Germany and then as an outsider in the West
after his emigration in 1980. The portfolio, *8
Erfahrungen*, which was acquired to demonstrate the
continuity of the German Expressionist woodcut
tradition, is preceded by the following preface from the
artist (in translation): 'The East has spewed me out/The
West has not yet devoured me/Now I throw my
experiences to the lions/Without the pride of Epictetus.'

PD 1983-6-25-34

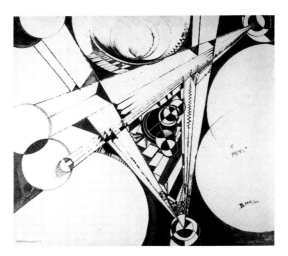

ROBERT MICHEL (1897–1983), **Zwischen Himmel und
Erde (Between Heaven and Earth)**, 1918. Black ink and
wash, 485 × 565 mm.

Michel, like many other progressive artists in Weimar
Germany, had an eclectic career, involving graphic and
architectural design as well as fine art. His early
compositions were influenced by his experience as a pilot
during World War I; a traumatic crash in 1917 left him
with a keen interest in the use of mechanical elements
as part of a cosmic vision.

PD 1983-4-16-1

institution exclusively concerned with display. One of the objectives, therefore, is to build up concentrations of work in particular fields which will provide a reasonable context for the study of as many aspects of a period as possible. The supercession of conventional printmaking techniques for reproductive purposes by photomechanical methods means that many former categories of printed material are no longer relevant to the twentieth-century collection, for example, portraiture, topography, historical series and caricature. This has had the effect of giving the fine art prints an overwhelming preponderance; nevertheless, subject matter and social context remain of importance. The department's character as a library collection has also had an influence on the physical shape of its contents. Ever since the establishment of the museum's first Print Room in 1808 the material has been housed as a cabinet of prints and drawings according to five standard sizes, with only limited provision for the storage of framed items.

František Kupka (1871–1957), **La Voie du Silence**, 1900–03. Etching and aquatint. 348 × 345 mm. Purchased from the Playfair Bequest.

Kupka, who settled in Paris in 1896 after training in Prague and Vienna, was to become one of the leading exponents of abstract colour theory. His early work, however, was very much preoccupied with metaphysical questions, influenced by the imagery of Edgar Allen Poe. He executed a small group of aquatints of this subject, varying the colour of the sky from blue to red to yellow, which relate to a pastel bearing the inscription 'Quam ad causum sumus' (Why are we here).

PD 1989–7–22–38

Heinrich Campendonk (1889–1957), **Half-nude with Cat**, 1912. Woodcut with watercolour, 284 × 284 mm (image size).

Campendonk was associated at this period with the Blaue Reiter group of artists around Franz Marc. Compositions such as this also reflect an awareness of Kokoshka's graphic work in Berlin, which was often reproduced in the journal *Der Sturm*.

PD 1988–12–10–7

Although this has not prevented the department from acquiring a number of large-scale works, the emphasis has had to rest on material which can be handled with relative ease.

In addition to the function described above, the department's policy is to maintain a programme of changing exhibitions almost entirely drawn from its own resources; after being shown in London these are frequently sent on tour elsewhere in the United Kingdom. The department regularly lends to exhibitions mounted by other institutions, which increasingly request twentieth-century items as the collection becomes better known. Within the modern field, exhibitions have served as an effective focus for collecting activities and as a vehicle for the publication of material once it has been acquired. Thus far the exhibitions have concentrated on print-making: *American Prints 1879–1979* in 1980, *The Print in Germany 1880–1933* in 1984,

LEOPOLDO MENDEZ (1903–1969), **The Symphonic Concert of Skeletons**, 1943. No 8 from an album of 25 woodcuts, numbered 46/50, 227 × 169 mm.

The album was published by the Taller de Grafica Popular in Mexico City, a co-operative workshop which Mendez had helped to found in 1937. This subject is a vivid example of the inventive use made by Mendez and his colleagues of the imagery traditionally associated with the 'Calaveras', satirical broadsheets issued for the festival of the Day of the Dead. It refers to the inaugural concert at the Bellas Artes in 1934, which aroused a protest on account of the high price of admission. The figure on the left is the artist, Diego Rivera, criticised here for his Trotskyist affiliations at the time.

PD 1990–11–9–140(8)

MILTON AVERY (1893–1965), **Night Nude**, 1953. Woodcut, 245 × 621 mm.

Although he was untutored in graphic techniques, the American painter Milton Avery proved to be a remarkably inventive printmaker, working in drypoint from 1933–49 and then in woodcut and monotype after a heart attack severely restricted his capacity to paint. *Night Nude* is the most subtle of all his woodcut images which he first printed in black alone, as is the case here, in an edition of 25, then in blue and black in an edition of 20.

PD 1981–7–25–13

ANA MARIA PACHECO (b. 1943), **Untitled**, 1991.
Charcoal, 738 × 640 mm.

Pacheco came from the interior of Brazil to study
sculpture at the Slade School of Art in 1973. Since then
she has developed a dramatic artistic vocabulary in her
sculpture, painting, drawing and printmaking, which is
greatly indebted to her Latin American background. This
is one of a group of drawings loosely based on the Biblical
characters of Judith and Salome which form part of the
artist's preparation for a set of ten new paintings.

PD 1991–5–11–21

Czechoslovak Prints from 1900 to 1970 in 1986
and *Avant-garde British Printmaking 1914–1960*
in 1990, a bias which reflects both the strength
of the existing holdings and the availability of
good material. However, just as much importance is attached to the acquisition of drawings;
the collection of British twentieth-century work
as a whole has been considerably improved,
while smaller groups of drawings have been put
together of the work of American, Canadian, German and other Continental European artists. In
order to emphasise its own interest in the field,
the department, in conjunction with the Museum
of Modern Art in New York, put on a special
exhibition in 1982 of *A Century of Modern Drawing*, from MoMA's collection.

The Department of Prints and Drawings does
not exist in isolation either from the rest of the
British Museum or from other collections in
London and beyond. It attempts, where possible,

Theodore Roszak (1907–1981), **Staten Island**, 1934
Lithograph, numbered 9/12, 320 × 425 mm.

Staten Island is a rare early example of colour lithography
by an American abstractionist; the small number of
impressions were printed by the artist himself, in different
colour variants. Roszak later made his reputation as a
sculptor, but during the 1930s he produced a body of
work which, like the composition here, often combined
spatial concepts assimilated from de Chirico with
elements of Bauhaus Constructivism and the futuristic
ideas of the American industrial designer, Norman Bel
Geddes.

PD 1988–10–1–36

to establish reciprocity with material elsewhere,
in the form of studies for particular objects, or
through a general community of interest in the
subject matter. Two groups of drawings by
Charles Rennie Mackintosh acquired in 1981
and 1984 can be juxtaposed with the Mackintosh
items in Medieval and Later Antiquities purchased between 1979 and 1983. The first of the
two groups had formerly belonged to Randolph
Schwabe, head of the Slade School of Art from
1930–1948; the drawings were offered to the
British Museum by private treaty sale in recognition of Schwabe's close links with the Print
Room. In 1981 the museum acquired one of nine
sketches known for Max Beckmann's painting
'Fastnacht', 1920; after the painting itself was
acquired by the Tate Gallery in the same year,
the museum purchased two further studies in

1984 in order to document more fully such an important picture in London. A group of works on paper by artists associated with the post-war CoBrA movement has recently been put together, just as the Tate has improved its representation of paintings in this area. The same has been done for contemporary German art with the drawings of Gerhard Richter, Anselm Kiefer and Markus Lupertz. On the other hand, the department no longer adds to its holding of posters or photographs, which are well represented by the Victoria and Albert Museum, while the acquisition of contemporary prints and books containing original prints is limited in deference to the far more comprehensive coverage of these areas at the V&A, the British Library and the Tate Gallery. In this way, the department of Prints and Drawings is one of a pool of interdependent resources for the study of twentieth-century art in London.

Frances Carey

ANSELM KIEFER (b. 1944), **'Dein goldenes Haar, Margarethe'**, 1981. Watercolour, 418 × 559 mm.

Kiefer's work has been replete with visual and literary metaphors for the psychological inheritance of modern Germany. In 1980 he began a series of paintings and watercolours inspired by 'Todesfuge' (Death Fugue), the most famous poem written by the Romanian author, Paul Celan, who lived in Paris from 1948 until his suicide in 1970. The poem, which was first published in 1952, deals obliquely with the Holocaust, using the words 'Your golden hair Margarethe' to represent an Aryan ideal of beauty, contrasting with the Semitic ideal 'Your ashen hair Shulamith'.

PD 1983–10–1–19

Bibliograpy of British Museum books relating to the twentieth century

Coins and Medals

PHILIP ATTWOOD
Acquisitions of Badges (1978–1982) Occasional Paper 55 1985

PHILIP ATTWOOD
Acquisitions of Badges (1983–1987) Occasional Paper 76 1990

*MARK JONES
The Dance of Death: German medals of the First World War 1978

*MARK JONES
Contemporary British Medals 1986

Ethnography

ELIZABETH CARMICHAEL and CHLOË SAYER
The Skeleton at the Feast: The Day of the Dead in Mexico, 1991

BRIAN DURRANS and ROBERT KNOX
India: Past into Present 1982

JOHN MACK
Madagascar: Island of the Ancestors 1986

JOHN MACK, Ed.
Ethnic Jewellery 1988

EDUARDO PAOLOZZI
Lost Magic Kingdoms 1985

JOHN PICTON and JOHN MACK
African Textiles 1989

MICHAEL O'HANLON
Reading the Skin 1989

CHLOË SAYER
Mexican Textiles 1990

SHELAGH WEIR
The Bedouin 1970, new ed. 1990

SHELAGH WEIR
Palestinian Costume 1989

SHELAGH WEIR and SERENE SHAHID
Palestinian Embroidery 1988

Oriental Antiquities

BARBARA BREND
Islamic Art 1991

S J VAINKER
Chinese Pottery and Porcelain: From Prehistory to the Present 1991

Japanese Antiquities

LAWRENCE SMITH
Contemporary Japanese Prints: Symbols of a Society in Transition 1985

*LAWRENCE SMITH
The Japanese Print Since 1900: Old Dreams and New Visions 1983

LAWRENCE SMITH, VICTOR HARRIS and TIMOTHY CLARK
Japanese Art: Masterpieces in the British Museum 1990. (Contains a chapter on twentieth-century prints.)

Medieval and Later Antiquities

MICHAEL COLLINS
Towards Post-Modernism: Design Since 1851 1987

CHARLOTTE GERE, JUDY RUDOE, HUGH TAIT and TIMOTHY WILSON, edited by HUGH TAIT
The Art of the Jeweller: A Catalogue of the Hull Grundy Gift to the British Museum: Jewellery, Engraved Gems and Goldsmiths' Work (2 vols) 1984

A G RANDALL,
Revised by RICHARD GOOD
Catalogue of Watches in the British Museum. Volume VI: Pocket Chronometers, Marine Chronometers and Other Portable Precision Timekeepers 1989

JUDY RUDOE
Decorative Arts 1850–1950: A Catalogue of the British Museum Collection 1991

Prints and Drawings

FRANCES CAREY, Ed.
Henry Moore: A Shelter Sketchbook 1988

*FRANCES CAREY and ANTONY GRIFFITHS
American Prints 1879–1979 1980

*FRANCES CAREY and ANTONY GRIFFITHS
The Print in Germany 1880–1933 1984

FRANCES CAREY and ANTONY GRIFFITHS
Avant-Garde British Printmaking, 1914–60 1990

*IRINA GOLDSCHEIDER
Czechoslovak Prints from 1900–70 1985

*BERNICE ROSE
A Century of Modern Drawing from the Museum of Modern Art, New York 1982

General

HENRY MOORE
Henry Moore at the British Museum 1981

Titles marked with a * were out of print at the time of writing, but may be available in libraries.